A LIFE TO DIE FOR

A LIFE TO DIE FOR

DISCOVERING YOUR PART IN GOD'S STORY

Andy Peck

THANKS

Writing a book is rarely a solitary project, and this one is no exception.

I want to thank those who have read part or all of the draft manuscript: Grace Benson, a colleague from Premier Media Group when I was at *Christianity* magazine, who was the first to read the early chapters and encouraged me to carry on, and Claire Stewart, who read the whole manuscript and gave me some excellent feedback on what worked and what didn't.

Thanks, too, to John Buckeridge, Senior Editor of *Christianity* magazine, Martin Saunders, Editor of *Youthwork* and Celia Hyland, CCP Web Editor, all colleagues at CCP Ltd (Christian Communications Partnership), whose advice and prayers meant a great deal as I was starting this book. Also, my wife Nic, who read the early chapters, listened to my ideas and with whom playing a part in God's story is such a joy.

Finally, thanks to the team at CWR, whose expertise I now observe first-hand as a colleague.

CONTENTS

'I tell you the truth, unless a grain of wheat falls to the ground and dies, it remains only a single seed. But if it dies, it produces many seeds. The man who loves his life will lose it, while the man who hates his life in this world will keep it for eternal life.'

The words of Jesus recorded in John 12:24–25

INTRODUCTION

You get one shot at life. How is it going?

Many can relate to the words of the nineteenth-century American thinker, Henry David Thoreau: 'Most men lead lives of quiet desperation and go to the grave with the song still in them.' We live in a time when there is an acceptance in the West that we need to 'choose life', yet so many find 'life' is a disappointment.

The sad thing is that the movement born from a Man who promised life in all its fullness is characterised by sterility. In Western Europe many of its meeting places are seen as museums to a time when God was the flavour of the month. Many of its people have retreated from the exciting adventure their Master planned. There are some glorious exceptions, but many 'Christians' believe the world is getting worse and worse so their gatherings operate like monastic outposts. Others suffer from deep insecurity and so keep their heads down, fearing they will be found out. Deep down they have faith, but feel powerless to fight back against the tide of anti-religious sentiment.

Many more adherents to Christianity elect champions who they believe will do battle for them: the pastor, the vicar, an apostle, an evangelist. They live their life through the surrogate activity of their leader and escape into mediocrity, believing that because their heroes are doing the business they can live in their slipstream.

But Jesus really meant it when He said He had come to give us 'life … to the full' (John 10:10). It was for anyone who followed Him, not just an elite. When the apostle Paul wrote of the inexpressible riches of God's love to us in Christ, he was inspired and he meant it (Eph. 3:8).

What if you discovered that all the books, courses and teaching about how you can have a great life pale into insignificance when compared to God's book? God's book tells a story in which humans find that helping themselves is incredibly short-sighted when the riches of God can be enjoyed. This is a God who tells it how it is and still loves you; who changes you to become who you always wanted to be but couldn't imagine in your wildest dreams.

What if some theologians and church leaders hide these facts from their readers and listeners because they can't quite believe the truths themselves? God bless every anointed preacher and leader who serves tirelessly, but it is God's intention that they equip you to serve. What if you could be sure that you have a part to play in the story God is writing?

Four years serving with a student movement in the UK and a further seven years in supported ministry in three churches, demonstrated to me that a small fraction of people in churches are actually living their part in God's story. For all the excellent changes in church life in the last fifty years – which include valuing the spiritual gifts of every church member and affirming the value of daily work – most Christians do not see themselves as part of God's story. Self-consciously they are defined by their job titles or major roles. They are a student, a housewife, househusband or retired, not apprentices to the most exciting Man to walk this planet. It is my assertion that you can find your part in God's story, and when you do it will blow your mind. God is extraordinarily good, better than you realise and can imagine.

If you don't know God you will have some work to do to vault some mindset barriers set against God. You aren't alone if you believe the negative publicity about God. This book invites you to do some hard thinking about what the Bible says. It's worth it.

If you do know God, this book will give you a fresh look at your relationship with Him. New life in Jesus remains the greatest news ever. Maybe you can get to know Him better and know more of His involvement with you in the life you are leading.

Perhaps you are tired of the Christianity you have practised. You know you are in first gear when it comes to your life in God. You believe you will be safely in heaven when you die and are immensely grateful, but you struggle with the business of living out your faith. You feel perpetually guilty that you are not reading the Bible more, praying more, witnessing more, giving more, but somehow you can't make the necessary changes.

Maybe you are sick of 'willpower-focused Christianity', which is effectively disengaged from the heart. It all seems such hard work! You admire those who practise it – their determination is very impressive – but you don't actually want to be like them. Not for a second.

Or are you Christian leader who experiences a sick feeling in the pit of your stomach as you contemplate another ten, twenty, thirty years of ministry the way you have always done it? You are one of the 50 per cent who has seriously considered quitting.[1]

Whatever category you fall into, you don't want to be presented with false hopes, least of all in a book. But what if a fresh look at Christianity the way Jesus intended it to be lived can help you rethink your faith, or find one that transforms your life? Jesus promises an easy yoke and a life that is attractive, joyful and free. A life to die for.

This book aims to introduce you to that kind of life. It's a new kind of life that is found in Jesus and it really is good news. God can be trusted.

The thinking enshrined in this book has been shaped by many people. One was John Ortberg, then Teaching Pastor at Willow Creek Community Church. In a throwaway remark on a tape I was listening to, he said we were to 'call people to live the life we were living'. The remark cut to my heart. I can remember where I was when I heard it – in a car outside a fitness centre in Southampton. Could I really do what he was suggesting?

I discovered that some of Ortberg's thinking stemmed from the writings of Dallas Willard. Willard's books opened my mind and heart to fresh thinking, rooted firmly in a Bible I thought I knew.[2] The books came at the right time, meshing together a deep and abiding appreciation of the Bible and reasoned and clear appreciation of the Spirit, with a clear vision of how Jesus actually intends us to grow.

My first book, *Coached by Christ*, looked at how, in the Gospels, Jesus coached His first twelve followers, and how He coaches us today. The book you now have in your hands draws from the whole Bible and looks more specifically at what Jesus is intending for us.

I believe the Bible is the Word of God and our final authority for faith and conduct, a belief shared by many mainstream denominations and new church streams in the UK. The style of this book means I don't necessarily 'show my working' when outlining advice. There will be many times when I will take a sentence or paragraph from a book in the Bible to indicate where you would find backing for my viewpoint. I have done my best to interpret well, but do please check the verses out for yourself.

How to read this book

Your time is precious. Having set aside time to read this book, you will want to know that it is going to be time well spent. There are no guarantees, but my goal as author is to ensure that what is of value to you will stay with you beyond the time we spend together.

Too often I have finished a book that seemed beneficial as I was reading it, only to realise a month or two later that it hadn't made the practical difference to my life that I had hoped for. An inability to recollect the details of a book or practise its lessons doesn't necessarily mean the book hasn't been of benefit. Ideas may be lodged in the subconscious, ready for use just when you need them. In my experience, however, this is all too rare – as rare as the times you keep a spare plug or screw for when you will need it, and then actually locate it when the occasion arises.

So, to get the maximum benefit from this book, have the mindset that it is not going to be 'another book I read once and then put back on the shelf'. I dare to believe that God is with you as you read and has ways for you to move forward that will change things for the better. Read this book with a notebook beside you, or make notes in the margin so you don't forget important points.

If you wouldn't call yourself a Christian, I hope that the first two chapters will give you a sufficient introduction to the faith for you to want to embrace it for yourself. Even if you are a believer, please read these chapters too as they will explain where I am coming from and offer a foundation for all that follows.

I hope you enjoy the ride.

Notes

1. Results from a survey of pastors, conducted by CWR and the Evangelical Alliance.
2. *The Spirit of the Disciplines* (HarperCollins, 1990), *Hearing God* (IVP, 1999), *The Divine Conspiracy* (HarperCollins, 1998) and *Renovation of the Heart in Daily Practice* (IVP, 2004). All are excellent. I recommend that you start with *The Divine Conspiracy*.
3. Andy Peck, *Coached by Christ* (CWR, 2005).

PROLOGUE

Any writer worth his salt will be aware that there is one thing he must do to keep his readers or viewers interested in his story: he must create conflict and tension within the narrative. If people don't care about what's happening, or they get bored, they will put the book down, change the TV channel or fall asleep in the cinema.

In films, one of the key ways of creating tension is to provide the viewer with information that the characters do not have, but would change everything if they did. In the case of *The Truman Show*, screenwriter Andrew Niccol engages his audience with a monumental fabrication. The main character, Truman Burbank, played by Jim Carrey, is chosen at birth from one of five unwanted babies to be the star of a continuously running reality TV show. Truman lives in an artificial town called Seahaven, which is located in a gigantic dome, and he grows up as the only person in the town who is unaware that he is living in a constructed reality for the entertainment of those outside. His friends, wife and family pretend to be friends with Truman, and in the case of his 'wife', conceal their real feelings of disgust.

The movie reaches a point where the producer of the show, Christof, played by Ed Harris, acknowledges that he has orchestrated Truman's entire life and now intends for him to father a baby – 'the first on-air conception'. He says that the reason Truman has never discovered the truth about his life is simple: 'We accept the world with which we're presented.' He believes Truman simply does not want to discover the truth – that he enjoys what he calls his 'prison cell', and will never leave. In fact, in true Hollywood style, Truman *does* discover the truth, proves Christof wrong by leaving the show, and becomes an 'inspiration' for TV viewers around the world.

Imagine – your whole life lived unaware of a truth that would change everything. Christof had a point: we do accept the world with which we are presented. In part, we have to. Our basic looks are pre-determined for us: you had no choice about whether your parents looked like Brad Pitt and Angelina Jolie or Woody Allen and Dame Edna Everage. You didn't decide on your siblings or wider family; whether your home was in the town centre, in the suburbs or in the countryside. You didn't decide whether you are quick over 100m; prefer jazz music to classical; can stomach oysters; prefer to use your right or left hand; have an eye for Picasso or are tone deaf.

But as well as accepting these aspects of our lives we have also 'accepted' a world-view – a way of looking at things, created by our culture and relationships with parents, siblings and peer groups. Richard J. Mouw, President at Fuller Theological Seminary and Professor of Christian Philosophy, says that a world-view is a way of answering four basic questions: 'Where are we?', 'Who are we?', 'What's wrong?' and 'What's the remedy?'[1] He says that all of us have a world-view, whether or not we think about it or articulate it. In other words, there are no neutral persons.

For most people in the West, God plays little or no practical role in the resolution of these questions in their lives. We may have listened to some insights in RE at school, but there was little or no expectation that God was anything more than a philosophical idea that religious leaders argued about. Certainly no careers advisor would ask whether we had considered God's purposes for our lives. If, along the way, we had a vague notion that fate or destiny – 'Truman style' – was orchestrating our life, it wasn't necessarily pleasant or comforting because we didn't know where it was leading.

So, for many people there is a creative tension in their personal story – a gap between knowing certain things about life and having major questions about where life is heading.

Christianity claims to hold the truth that changes everything. It flows out of God's story – a narrative that takes us from the very first humans to the end of time itself, which will include us within it if we ask to be counted in. God's story is outlined in the sixty-six books of the Bible and continues to be applied in His ongoing work in the Christian Church down through the centuries. God's story answers major questions for us, enabling the gates of our prison cells to be burst wide open. If we accept the answers, we are never the same again.

You will have guessed from the title of the book that I believe that life does have purpose and meaning because the God who made it is personal and loving and calls each of us to join with Him in His good purposes for the world. I believe you can know your part in God's story: God wants to incorporate you into what He is doing. This is stunning, life-changing information that can break into anyone's individual storyline and set it on a completely different footing – rather like realising that you are permanently on TV.

Not discovered your role yet?

If Christianity is so great, why do so many Christians live far below God's good intentions for them? There are many reasons:

- Some don't expect any sort of part in God's story. They believe that trusting Jesus is all they need to do. Heaven is assured, they just need to wait.
- Many are frightened about what God might want of them. They think their lifestyle or friends or leisure pursuits would need to change if they were to become more committed.
- Some have tasted the part that God wants them to play but believe they are out of the game because they have let God down.
- Many are sitting back, waiting for God to tell them what He wants, but don't seem to find an answer.
- Many are desperate to discover God's part for them but are at a loss to know what they need to do.

If you find you have a hazy view about what God may have in mind for you and feel uncommitted to the cause, you are in good company: Jesus' early followers were not much further on in their thinking when they started out, and remained perplexed even after spending three years in Jesus' company. What they did discover, however, and what we need to discover, is that God is good, that His purposes for us are good and that we are missing out if we opt for a Christianity without knowing God's story and playing our part in it.

Like Truman, we need to grasp that the framework of life is not what we thought: we need to see our lives and our world through God's eyes and not the more limiting perspective we may have imbibed from the culture around us. In short, we need to discover the stage God has set for us and what this means for us.

Note

1. Richard J. Mouw, 'And Grace Will Lead Us Home: The Old-Time Religion for a New Millennium', speech given at The Chautauqua Institution, Chautauqua, New York, July 1999.

01
SET THE STAGE

SET THE STAGE

You find your part in God's story when you see the world the way God sees it. This is the stage on which your life can be lived. It's a great place to get to know God, and there's more to come.

Tracing ancestors is a piece of cake on the Internet. Brits no longer have to tramp up to Somerset House in London to leaf through the public records of wills, birth certificates and so on, or hire an investigator. They are just a few mouse clicks away from locating all manner of great-great-great-aunts, -uncles and grandparents they didn't know they had. It's fascinating to see whether anyone exciting, famous or notorious lurks in the family tree. In the UK, two TV channels picked up on this epidemic of ancestor research by commissioning programmes showing celebrities discovering their roots, with *Who Do You Think You Are?* (BBC) and *You Don't Know You're Born* (ITV). For some it is deeply emotional stuff: the robust hard-man broadcast journalist, Jeremy Paxman, wept at the indignity suffered by an ancestor condemned to live in a Victorian workhouse. BBC newsreader, Natasha Kaplinski, was moved to learn that one of her relatives narrowly escaped a massacre of 2,700 Polish Jews, wiped out in a single day during World War II.

Finding your part in God's story[1] also involves investigating a family. Those exploring Christianity look in on God's family, as described in the Bible and displayed in the Christian Church, and wonder if they would like to be part of it. Those already committed to Christianity discover their family history is richer and more diverse than they ever imagined: they have spiritual ancestors in Scripture who are exciting, famous and notorious; people who, often despite little natural advantage and appallingly low moral character, were raised up by God to play significant roles in His glorious adventure. These predecessors serve as an inspiration to Christians to play their part in God's story wherever He has placed them today.

God's family recorded in Scripture is unique in the way that the characters viewed the world. After all, God interacted with its members, taught them about Himself and inspired a written record to be kept for generations to come. They were not imprisoned in their thinking – 'Truman style' (as we saw in the Prologue) – but were released to see life through God's eyes, with their hopes and dreams as big and as positive as God Himself. They provide a model for all today who want to know how this same God can work with them in the world. There are many dimensions to their outlook – here are the five main ones to set the stage for the part you and I can play in what God is doing.

1. It is God's story

It was the pastor and author, A.W. Tozer, who said that what comes into our minds when we think about God is the most important thing about us.[2] As soon as you see the word 'God' on a page you make some sort of reaction.

The Bible reveals God as an eternal Spirit who has created all that is; who has made us to be like Him; who loves us and the world passionately; and who wants the very best for us. The God of the Bible, when properly understood, inspires thoughts of awe, delight, love, gratitude, worship and holy fear. God has always existed as Father, Son and Holy Spirit. These three are a community of Persons who love each other, delight in each other and need nothing and no one to complete who they are and what they do.

The Bible tells us that God chose to create a world with humans in it who would love and know Him and explore and occupy a fantastic creation fitted for their enjoyment and delight. The world's beauty and wonder, joy and delight, variety and bounty are a sign of God's power and glory (Psa. 95; Rom. 1:20). A God who creates the duck-billed platypus, the giraffe and the hippopotamus has great ingenuity and a sense of humour. The many who care about nature and value its richness care about what God has made, even if they don't give Him credit as the Creator.

The first humans, Adam and Eve, were created, placed in a beautiful garden and given the opportunity to enjoy all that God had made, in friendship with Him. The community of Father, Son and Spirit shared its love with others. Adam and Eve were told to take charge of the world for God in interaction with Him and, within certain boundaries, could do as they pleased. It was perfect. God created love, joy, peace, sex, laughter, excitement, passion and satisfaction to be part of the human experience. Whatever you can imagine as being the very best in life would be a fraction of what God desires for His world and those in it.

There was one boundary. Adam and Eve were told they were not to eat the fruit from the tree of the knowledge of good and evil, and that if they ate it they would die. Just one rule, given for their good. But they disobeyed the command. Through this act of disobedience they became separate from God, a separation the Bible describes as spiritual death. This was followed later by physical death – part of God's judgment, but also His kindness: now that sin had entered the world, the process of decay would be unbearable if humans were to live too long in a physical body.

God's splendour is enhanced when we see His response to all this. He could have wiped humanity out, but such is His nature that He sets out to right the wrong and bring us back from the brink. The narrative of the Bible tells the story of how God, the loving Creator, woos humans back to Himself even after they turn their backs on Him. We are like the lover who leaves her family home, sleeps around, slanders her husband, disgraces his name, spends his fortune, but who is still welcomed back if she will just recognise her folly. The overtures of love continue until her stubborn heart finally breaks.

If you don't know God yet, this might all seem a very fanciful idea which begs the question: If this is God's story, why do so many claim never to have met Him – why does He seem so silent and impotent? And why do so many believe in gods other than the God of the Bible?

God's apparent hiddenness is part of His loving care – His way of protecting us. If we were to meet Him in His glory it would be like the power of the national grid being connected to a toaster. One of the reasons for the coming of 'God-the-Son' to earth was that Jesus could provide a safe connection between God and us. We can approach God because of what Jesus did for us in His death, resurrection and ascension.

That is not to say that God, by His Spirit, cannot be close to each one of us. If we have any concept of God we may imagine that He is somewhere beyond the solar system. In fact, in Matthew's Gospel,

Jesus talks of God's rule and reign as the 'kingdom of heaven', literally 'kingdom of the heavens'. The Jews believed in three heavens: the first heaven was the atmosphere, the second was the stars and the third was the home of the angels. Jesus was saying that God's kingdom is as close as the air around us.[3] God is potentially *that* close. You can't see Him, but, as Paul says to the Greeks in Athens, 'he is not far from each one of us' (Acts 17:27).

In fact, the Bible says that everyone knows instinctively that there is a God. Our conscience and the world around us speak of a divine 'someone' who put everything together. And we have a written library of sixty-six books ('Bible' means 'library') to chart His faithful and loving pursuit of people such as you and me.

Despite God's power and majesty He is not 'in your face'. You have a measure of freedom in life and even at this moment can choose to reject His loving overtures or even tell yourself that you would rather believe in another god, or no god. But that would be total folly, like throwing away a winning lottery ticket. We can join with God's story as willing participants in what He is doing; for not only does He lovingly pursue humanity, He has chosen to partner with people like you and me.[4] Which brings us to the second part of the story:

2. It was always intended that we partner with God

God allowed our first parents, Adam and Eve, enormous freedom. They were given the world to subdue and manage under His loving rule. That is what it means to be human – managing and ruling are standard functions for *homo sapiens*! We were 'made in the image of God' (Gen. 1:27–28). Just as a human parent dotes over a baby who has his or her characteristics, so God, as it were, 'dotes' over us. Theologians have puzzled over what being made in God's image actually means, but most conclude that it refers to the fact that we are given many of God's key characteristics. Like God, we are spiritual, personal, thinking, feeling, choosing, creative beings designed to make a difference within our world. And we do this by knowing and working with God. Some may feel they are more brain than heart, or more body than creative spark, but all of us have some measure of each.

As university professor and author, Dallas Willard, puts it: 'We are, all of us, never-ceasing spiritual beings with a unique eternal calling to count for good in God's great universe.'[5] We are not physical beings trying to have a spiritual experience, but spiritual beings with a physical experience, which will continue beyond this world.

Knowing that you are made by God makes sense of the desires you have so that they count for something in life. Your family, friends, peer group, society or nation may have let you down in some way, but God places a high value on you – you matter to Him. God knows your number, name and address. Your life is a gift and you can have purpose, excitement and adventure as you get to know what is possible in partnership with Him. Living without God is like drawing using a lead pencil when you could be painting in colour, or travelling on a bike when you could be in a limousine. God is the 'X-factor' par excellence, who can transform anyone and any situation.

South African statesman, Nelson Mandela, wrote of our potential:

> *Our deepest fear is not that we are inadequate. Our deepest fear is that we are powerful beyond measure. It is our light, not our darkness that most frightens us. We ask ourselves, Who am I to be brilliant, gorgeous, talented, fabulous? Actually, who are you not to be? You are a child of God. Your playing small does not serve the world. There is nothing enlightened about shrinking so that other people won't feel insecure around you. We are all meant to shine, as children do. We were born to make manifest the glory of God that is within us. It's not just in some of us; it's in everyone. And as we let our own light shine, we unconsciously give other people permission to do the same. As we are liberated from our own fear, our presence automatically liberates others.*[6]

God is keen that you fully exhibit all the facets of the nature He has given you, but without the sinful tendencies that hold you back. Mandela is partly correct. Yes, God's glory is in us, but sin has marred God's design. Those who are discovering their part in what God is doing see the folly of paths and projects that don't fit in with His big picture for them. They rejoice that each day is a fresh opportunity to experience more of God in His world.

Shortly we will look at how 'God-the-Son', Jesus Christ, enables us to enter into God's story, but here we will merely note that all the potential for playing a role in God's world is already within you. You are the rusty engine awaiting a mechanic, the ruin needing restoration, the trained athlete needing a medical team to mend his legs ready to sprint once again.

3. Jesus is the leading Player

We have seen already that God is three Persons: Father, Son and Holy Spirit (known as the Trinity, or the Godhead). Each Member has distinct roles within the team, but the same personality. When any one is at work, you can be sure that the other two are in agreement. The New Testament outlines the massive ramifications of the coming of 'God-the-Son' to earth as a human being and how as a result of His life, death, resurrection and ascension, the Godhead has made Jesus the Master of the universe. He has total power over it, a power He wields benevolently and according to His Father's wishes, and largely through His people as they trust Him and can be trusted to use what He offers. Everyone will see that power when He returns to execute judgment on this world and take His followers to be with Him.

However, the way in which Jesus became the leading Player was not pain-free. One of the best-known verses in the Bible, John 3:16, sums it up: 'For God so loved the world that he gave his one and only Son, that whoever believes in him shall not perish but have eternal life.' Not only did God-the-Son leave the throne of heaven to become human, but also His humanity led to agony at the heart of the Godhead as the Son died for the sins of the world.

That's a big claim which needs explaining. Jesus' death came at the hands of Jewish leaders who were jealous of His popularity and angry at what they perceived to be His blasphemous teaching. They convinced a weak Roman governor to put Him to death for no just reason. Both the Father and the Son had chosen this act as the means by which Jesus would bear the punishment due to a rebellious world. In His death, Jesus willingly suffered the just anger of God against sin, knowing that

His sacrifice would enable those who put their confidence in Him to be counted as righteous before God.

Just when evil appeared to have triumphed, Jesus was raised from the dead – three days after He was put in the tomb. He had no reason to remain dead for He had never sinned. In raising Him, His Father was confirming the acceptance of His sacrifice and fulfilling His promise to bring new life to His people. And so, much to their surprise (despite His predictions), Jesus appears to His followers to confirm the truth of all they had been hearing during their three years with Him. He then briefed them on the next stage of God's purposes.

Later, the apostle Paul, the foremost theologian of the early followers, would say of Jesus:

> *He is the image of the invisible God, the firstborn over all creation. For by him all things were created: things in heaven and on earth, visible and invisible, whether thrones or powers or rulers or authorities; all things were created by him and for him.*
>
> Col. 1:15–16

Paul also wrote:

> *Therefore God exalted him to the highest place and gave him the name that is above every name, that at the name of Jesus every knee should bow, in heaven and on earth and under the earth, and every tongue confess that Jesus Christ is Lord, to the glory of God the Father.*
>
> Phil. 2:9–10

The impact of Jesus on world history is unparalleled. The events of His life were so defining that nations would come to mark every year in history in reference to years before or since His coming ('BC' means 'Before Christ' and 'AD' stands for 'Anno Domini', translated 'in the year of our Lord'). Today, one third of the world claims some allegiance to Jesus, and many have discovered that He does indeed live up to His billing as Master of the universe. It has been said that 'history' is 'His story', which may sound a touch corny but reflects accurately the sort of drama of which we are part.

Throughout history, God's people, who find their part in God's story, become impressed with Jesus Christ and find Him to be the world's leading Player: the wisest, most heroic, most faithful, competent, intelligent Leader ever to have walked this earth. Whether you are six or ninety-six, it is not too late to link in with His purposes and make your days, weeks, months and years count.

4. We are invited to live a new kind of life

Jesus, the leading Player, invites us to learn from Him how to partner with God in the same way He did. We have great potential (as we noted in the second point on page 24), but our human nature trips us up: deep down we are rebels against God, unable and unwilling to change.

When Jesus came He said to His people (and all of humanity), effectively: *You can join Me in living under the rule and reign of My Father in His kingdom. This is what you were made for. Rely on Me and I will show you how to live.*

God created human nature so that each of us has a 'kingdom': a part of life that we have a say over. You see this in toddlers, gradually exercising their 'will' and deciding just what they want. As they grow up, this kingdom expands from being their choice in clothes or how they arrange their bedroom, to, as adults, how they control their homes, garden or company. God, too, has a kingdom. In His kingdom, what He wants done is done. It incorporates the natural world and the lives of those who choose to be part of His story.[7]

God's desire is that we choose to put our kingdoms into His, but He will not force us to. When we consider our kingdoms, one thing is clear – we are not very good managers. We may seem to do OK, but we struggle because we are running our kingdoms independent of God's. Not only do we miss out on being part of what He is doing, but we also face physical death alone and an eternity without any of the glorious possibilities God plans for those who are part of what He intends. This place of separation from God is what the Bible calls 'hell'.

God's kingdom is stunning. Jesus, anointed by the Holy Spirit, is able to demonstrate the reality of the kingdom, as His Father directs

Him. The sick are healed, the blind see. Jesus has power over the wind and the waves. He can change the molecular structure of water to make it mature wine. He even reverses the death and decay in a widow's son, a young girl and a close friend. As people voluntarily came to Him, they knew the action of God in their lives.

However, living in the kingdom was not about having a miracle a day. Jesus' taught His special followers how to live under God's reign as He did. This has been so misunderstood by Christians that it is worth underlining. Jesus does not tell us that living a new kind of life means that we try to be good. He doesn't even say, *Trust in My death and resurrection to save you and then try to be good.* He says: *Rely on Me by trusting what I say about life.* This means learning from Him how to live: loving family and friends, caring for others, curbing temper, controlling lust, promoting peace and joy, enhancing others' lives, acting fairly, being generous. The sort of good life we long to live at our very best moments that makes us a blessing to be with and has a positive impact on society. In due course Jesus will take care of death too. As author Dallas Willard so memorably puts it: 'I am learning from Jesus how to live my life as He would live it if He were me.'[8]

This, then, is the invitation; not a passport to 'the other side', but an invitation to life now. The only definition of eternal life in the whole Bible says, 'Now this is eternal life: that they may know you, the only true God, and Jesus Christ, whom you have sent' (John 17:3). The word 'know' in this context means 'interactive relationship'. Those who play their part in God's story accept Jesus' invitation into the dramatic action of God. They learn to be a force for good in the world, seeing His supernatural activity in the lives of people, transforming their hearts and minds to live for God. They see tangible evidence of Him at work as He transforms the world; work that will continue until the day He finally winds up history and welcomes home all who know and love Him. We will be welcomed into a new heaven and a new earth where we will joyfully enter into all that God has for us. We are not obliged to accept this invitation, but what is on offer is so exciting that if we really grasped it we would know that nothing else would do. We look in more detail at how we join with Jesus in Chapter 2.

5. Evil has a source and will be overcome

Many may be aghast at the picture I have painted so far. I recall a work colleague many years ago ridiculing the idea that God was working out His purposes in our world. Evil was so rampant, he said, that he couldn't accept that there was a divine being who was at work at all. If God was all-powerful, why didn't He step in and right the wrongs? My former colleague isn't alone in his opinion; spend any time watching TV news channels or thumbing through the daily newspaper and you can become thoroughly depressed by world events.

I cannot, in the space I have available here, pretend to do justice to the questions surrounding why God created a world in which evil and suffering are possible.[9] I can, however, briefly outline how evil entered the world and affirm again, that God is good, is at work in our world to overcome evil, and will triumph. This is part of the story of God.

It's clear from reading Genesis 1–3 and other passages, that God gives some of His creation – humans and angelic beings – a measure of freedom. It is the misuse of this freedom that is the cause of problems in the world. Angels are 'heavenly beings', spiritual in nature. We don't generally get to see them, but they enter our physical world as human-like beings from time to time. Initially an angelic being (known as Satan or the devil) sought to usurp God's authority around the time of the earth's creation and was thrown out from God's presence (heaven) because of his rebellion, taking other angels with him (see Isa. 14:12–14; Ezek. 28:12–17 and Rev 12:7–9). So, a real devil and real demonic forces who oppose God and His purposes exist in our world today.

Humans also are free to choose whether to live in relationship with God or not. Adam and Eve's decision to go their own way (eating the forbidden fruit and suffering the consequences of separation from God) has affected humanity ever since. There is now a barrier between humans and God. We are expelled from the garden and will, in time, suffer physical death. God's mandate to fill the earth and subdue it continues, and we are still made in His image (Gen. 9:6) but we are now inclined towards pursuing our own selfish ends, tending to defend our own turf and attack our opponents rather than live in harmony.

This explanation is uncomfortable to many because it asserts that humans are responsible for the mess in the world, and therefore we cannot look disapprovingly at the problems and tell God He doesn't know what He is doing. Have we never caused pain and suffering? Given the right circumstances, doesn't the monster lurk within us all? As descendants of Adam and Eve we have inherited their defiance, and separation from God remains our prospect too if we don't change tack. We can only start to play our part in God's story when we recognise that our own story, without Him, only has one ending – *eternity* without Him.

The entrance of evil into humanity had repercussions on our physical world too: lethal earthquakes, volcanoes and hurricanes are amongst the evidence of a world out of sync. Humans become susceptible to viruses and poisons. The animal, insect and plant kingdoms become a threat not a blessing.

However, those who play their part in God's story know that evil in the world will be overcome and can be overcome within their own lives. The story does not stop in Genesis 3; the sixty-six books in the Bible provide a compelling narrative of God's work in and through flesh-and-blood humanity, proving God to be the great God, able to turn lives around and bring beauty from despair. In the end evil is conquered, Satan is defeated and the story continues into the life to come.

Many Christians seem confused about the future. Both the apostle Peter (2 Pet. 3:13) and the apostle John (Rev. 21:1) write of a new heaven and new earth. In Revelation 21:3 we find that a new city, in which God dwells, will come down from heaven. The implication is that there is some continuity between this earth and the new renewed earth. We are not evacuated to heaven never to return. Those who have died trusting Jesus will have new bodies to take their place on the launch pad for God's next exciting instalment (Phil. 3:21) in a renewed earth. Our future is as thrilling and extraordinary as God Himself. Eternal life begins when we choose to involve ourselves with God, but we look forward to the day when faith will give way to sight and we join with all who have known God in this life to enjoy Him in the next.

If this sounds at all fanciful, remember that nearly 90 per cent of the promises of God in the Bible have already been fulfilled. Most were focused on Jesus' first coming, and not one that should have happened has failed to happen. Even a betting man might conclude that the other promises regarding the end of the world are odds-on certainties!

If you take your part in God's story it will last for the length of your earthly life, and then forever![10] This is a long-term and high-yielding investment. What else can you invest in which has eternal value? This view of the world assures those for whom life has been a disappointment that it is not too late to do something worthwhile, which really will last. And for others who have had a part in God's story, there is the reminder that if life has not necessarily produced awards and prizes, they may have accomplished more of lasting value than they realise.

Our assurance, that God's story is a story that has 'to be continued' at the end of every day, gives impetus to those who join with God. Jesus came to give life in all its fullness and promises to deliver, creating communities embodying His values and infecting the world with His goodness.

The stage is set

This, then, is the way people who know their part in God's story see life. It is a glorious setting in which to live – there's a freshness, a hope and an excitement in being taken up and made part of a fantastic narrative, led by Someone about whom you can have 100 per cent confidence. This is truth which can change everything.

The question that remains is whether you are ready to walk onto the stage and play the part God has for you. You may feel a long way away from doing it at the moment, or you may already warm to this world-view. But remember, in one hundred years' time, it will be decisions taken now, in the light of the new creation, that will really count.

Summary

1. God's family has a particular way of seeing the world.
2. This is God's story. The world is a place where God is alive, at work and will accomplish His glorious purposes against the tide of evil.

3.   Jesus is the Leader of the universe who invites us to learn to live a new kind of life.
4.   Evil has a source and will be overcome. Those who are part of God's story can be part of His restoration process.

Action

1.   Look at the five elements of God's story. How would your life be different if you really accepted how the stage was set?
2.   List what comes into your mind when you think about God. How different is it from the biblical view?
3.   List what you plan for your story. How much of this would be tough to give up?

Consider

1.   How much of God's story in the Bible are you aware of? How could you learn more?
2.   Does setting the stage in this way make sense of the world? Is there anything that doesn't fit?

Notes
1.   I am using the words 'God's story' to mean both the biblical story and the story of God's work in our world since Bible times. This is warranted by the Bible itself, which predicts the end of the world and expects Christ's followers to engage in the drama of life based on the stupendous events surrounding the life of Jesus – that means every day since the ascension of Jesus and the coming of the Spirit up to this day.
     I believe that the biblical story records real events and people I will one day meet in the new heavens and new earth. These records are backed by archeological finds, which match much of the biblical data. Historians' records of God's story in human history after the biblical era are enormously helpful, especially in their reflections on how the truth about the Bible and Jesus should be understood and interpreted today. But only

Scripture has authority to tell us about God, our world and how we should live within it.

This book doesn't go into much detail about the biblical story. To understand more about how the Bible narrative hangs together, see the brief outline in the Appendix. Also, I recommend *A Passion for God's Story* (Paternoster/CWR, 2003), by my colleague at CWR, Philip Greenslade, and *The Drama of Scripture* by Craig Bartholomew and Michael Goheen (SPCK, 2006).

2. A.W. Tozer, *The Knowledge of the Holy* (HarperSanFrancisco; Reissue edition 1978).

3. There is a tension between God's immanence and God's transcendence: God is both close to us and also distant. The Bible underlines that His holiness is such that human beings need a mediator if they are to be acceptable to Him. Many people presume that God is too distant to be interested in them. This image of the kingdom in the air around reminds us that God's action is not far away.

4. Scripture does teach that we are constrained in our actions by our sin bias and therefore need God's liberating work of grace. Our wills don't appear to be free. But, there are also plenty of occasions when God clearly calls on us to repent (eg, Acts 17:30) as if we are able to do so.

5. Dallas Willard, *The Divine Conspiracy* (HarperCollins, 1998).

6. Nelson Mandela, *Long Walk to Freedom* (Back Bay Books, 1995).

7. The Bible teaches that God upholds the universe by His Word. He has set up the amazing natural world with all its complexity. But we don't need to conclude that natural disasters must therefore reflect His direct purpose. The natural world was also affected by the Fall, and awaits the day when Jesus will return to restore and renew creation (Rom. 8:19–21).

8. Unpublished article, 'How Does the Disciple Live?', on Dallas Willard's website, www.dwillard.org

9. The Bible does not provide an answer as to why God created a world in which evil would be possible. It tells us that God is sovereign and we are responsible for the evil we perpetrate. Both assertions are true and one should not be stressed to the exclusion of the other. God does intervene in the world to stop evil and bring good from evil, but we are not privy to why He does this in some situations and not others. However, Christians know the character of God – that He loves the world and that He always does what is the very best. They trust that if there had been a better way, He would have arranged it. That may sound trite given the great evil we see in our world but, although not an exhaustive answer, I believe it is the best that fits the evidence.

10. Your story is written against the backdrop of the wider story of the Bible. It is helpful to see the unfolding drama of the Bible in six acts (I have based these on *The Drama of Scripture* by Craig Bartholomew and Michael Goheen, SPCK, 2006):

    Act 1: God establishes His kingdom – creation

    Act 2: Rebellion in the kingdom – the Fall

Act 3: The King chooses Israel – the kingdom initiated
Act 4: The coming of the King – redemption accomplished
Act 5: Spreading the news of the King – the mission of the Church
Act 6: The return of the King – redemption completed
We are in Act 5, with the opportunity to benefit from the news of the King. The drama of God's story will unfold one way or another, whether we choose to join in or not. But the ramifications of His story need checking out. If we can have an interactive relationship with the Creator of the universe, who wants our good and will direct our lives, then it is worth considering, if we haven't done so already.
See further outlines of the Bible in the Appendix.

02
JOIN WITH THE LEADING PLAYER

JOIN WITH THE LEADING PLAYER

You are able to play a part because Jesus, the leading Player in world history, makes it possible. He invites you to enjoy the benefits of being in His team.

If Christianity is as fantastic as was suggested in Chapter 1 then we need to make absolutely sure that we are part of God's story. But whereas joining most things in life has one agreed procedure, there are a multitude of ideas on how you join with Jesus:

- You pray the 'sinner's prayer', asking God to save you
- You show your seriousness by turning from your sin
- You receive a blessing from a priest
- You attach yourself to a local church
- You are confirmed and receive your first Communion
- You are baptised as an adult

What do people who claim to be Christians say? In the UK, the Census of England and Wales in 2005 found that 72 per cent of the population said that they were Christian. Yet very few of these ever attend a place of worship, with weekly figures averaging around 10 per cent. Are they 'in' because they say they are, or are there other criteria we should use? What of those who say they have joined with Jesus because Britain is a Christian country, or because they were baptised as an infant, or confirmed in the Church of England?

To answer this, we need to go back to the source documents themselves. If God is as concerned about us joining with Him as we suggested in Chapter 1, then you would think that He would have made it crystal clear in the Bible, even if His followers through the centuries have had disagreements. So what does it mean to join with Jesus and how could we go about it if we wanted to?

Joining with Jesus in the Gospels

As we saw in the previous chapter, when Jesus started His public ministry, aged around thirty, He travelled around Israel preaching to the people. Mark's Gospel begins with a summary of what Jesus was saying: The time has come, the kingdom of God is near, *'repent and believe the good news'* (Mark 1:15, my emphasis).

Jesus was saying that His hearers needed to be aware of an exciting development. They expected God's rule and reign to come when they died and entered 'the age to come' after this life. Jesus was saying that this rule could be known by relying on Him and His teaching now. It was time to change their minds about what life was like and accept the new state of affairs.

Some time ago a telecoms company phoned me to tell me that they had been conducting work in our area and had now made broadband available to our home. Instead of having to dial up for my Internet connection I could now be online 24/7. They alerted me to the fact that I had access to something that could make a change to my life. If I hadn't been told, there was no way I would have known. In the same way, Jesus was alerting people to the availability of the kingdom. He was saying, 'Did you know that you can have "kingdom access" through putting your confidence in me?' Except, of course, this is far more exciting. This is the equivalent of telling paupers that they have access to a continuous banquet – food, drink and luxurious housing forever.

This rule of God would become known as people learned from Jesus how God intended them to live. It is a transformation from people looking after no.1 to trusting in God to look after them. Alongside the life-changing teaching is proof of His Father's love for people as the effects of sin and evil are reversed: for example, the blind are able to see, the lame walk, the deaf hear – God is showing that He is on people's side.

The 'repent' word in Mark's summary above is not as alarming as it sounds. For many, the word 'repent' creates an image of a man outside a football ground wearing a billboard, or a preacher with a black Bible wagging his finger and telling people how bad they are. But 'repent' merely means 'change your mind' – you might repent over whether you wanted to eat at a particular fast-food outlet, or whether your sports team was going to have a good season. Jesus did not travel round Israel condemning people for their sin, but opened up the way for people to know God, and then they would find that sin was not nearly so attractive. In following His way they would know how to live in dependence on Him now and, as He promised (through His death and resurrection), would enjoy life beyond death too.

Jesus invited particular people to be on a special fast-track apprenticeship scheme with Him. Twelve men were chosen to spend time with and learn from Him for the next stage of God's timetable, after Jesus' return to heaven. It involved followers of Jesus extending the offer of living under God's rule to the rest of the world.

But the invitation to learn how to live in God's kingdom was open to all: to the religious and the non-religious, to those who had a daily time in the Torah and those who had given up on any sort of Scripture reading. It came to those who thought God had a downer on them and those who were convinced that they were in His good books. He taught in public from village to village and crowds followed. The Sermon on the Mount is directed at His own team (Matt. 5:1) but attracted hundreds of people who listened in (Matt. 7:28). There was no need for a ticket, though you might have found the teaching so compelling that you needed a miracle to feed you (see Matt. 14:13–21).

So, Jesus' call to repent and believe the good news meant the believer realising that God was now acting in human history again, fulfilling the Old Testament prophets' predictions of a Messiah who would come as a rescuer, and choosing to align themselves with this new movement by turning from sin to follow Him. You learn to rely on Him and are promised life in the life to come.[1]

Some had an initial interest in Jesus – partly because they saw the miracles – but then drifted away when they realised what He was talking about. Certainly you could opt out if you wished, though Jesus is adamant that if you really grasp what is going on you would be spoilt for anything else.

In John's Gospel, Jesus tells one of the Jewish leaders that 'no-one can see the kingdom of God unless he is born again' (John 3:3). 'Born again' literally means 'born from above' and is a metaphor for the new life that comes to His followers. The phrase has been cheapened in the modern day by people who want to give certain types of Christians a 'born again' tag. In fact, by definition, any true Christian is born again

– using it as an adjective is like speaking of a 'colourful' rainbow or a 'reflecting' mirror. It gloriously signifies the action of God in making a new people who have finished writing their story their way and begun with God, entering His story by linking with the leading Player, and becoming part of the family He is building.[2]

Repentance, trust and the associated idea of being born again, signified the new kind of life that Jesus was offering. But that was then. Jesus is no longer physically available to join with people. What happened when He left?

Joining with Jesus in the book of Acts

As we saw in the previous chapter, Jesus' coming represented a monumental change in the history of the world. James Burke, the scientific journalist, wrote a book, *The Day the Universe Changed*, to describe how an invention or discovery had monumental ramifications for society. If such a book were written about Jesus we might call it, 'The Days the Universe Changed'. The death, resurrection, ascension and subsequent sending of the Spirit (taking place in a period of just under two months) changed our universe, leading to the birth of the Christian Church, a movement that is still alive in your town today.

The book of Acts is the record of how the early followers continued what Jesus had started by inviting people to join with Him. It covers His return to heaven and ends in the mid-60s AD when one of the main players, Paul, is under house arrest, awaiting trial in Rome. Jesus is not physically present but still acts by His Spirit within the narrative. The apostles tell people that, in view of what Jesus has now done on humankind's behalf, they should change their thinking and behaviour. If Jesus is the Master of the universe then it is time to stop running life as if He isn't. He provides forgiveness and new life, which now continues beyond the grave.

Peter, one of His closest followers, having been empowered by the Holy Spirit, says at the end of his sermon to 3,000-plus on the Day of Pentecost:

'Therefore let all Israel be assured of this: God has made this Jesus,

whom you crucified, both Lord and Christ.
When the people heard this, they were cut to the heart and said to
Peter and the other apostles, 'Brothers, what shall we do?' Peter
*replied, '***Repent and be baptised***, every one of you, in the name*
of Jesus Christ for the forgiveness of your sins. And you will receive
the gift of the Holy Spirit.'

Acts 2:36–38, my emphasis

Later, another Early Church leader, the apostle Paul, would have an opportunity to address leaders in Athens. Towards the end of his message, referring to their idolatry, he says:

'In the past God overlooked such ignorance, but now he commands
*all people everywhere ***to repent***. For he has set a day when he will*
judge the world with justice by the man he has appointed. He has
given proof of this to all men by raising him from the dead.'

Acts 17:30–31, my emphasis

The Athenians had no heritage of belief in God, but were told they must re-think their view of life in the light of the resurrection, ascension and return of Jesus.

Here, as throughout the New Testament, the apostles teach that the truths about Jesus are of such major importance in life that nothing else matters anymore. Grasping this is like receiving the news that you are to inherit a million pounds, or about to be a parent, or that the disease you thought was killing you isn't. It is life-changing and you cannot think about life in the same way again.

Joining with Jesus today

You join with Jesus today in the same way that people joined with Jesus in the New Testament after He left this earth. These illustrations are not ancient history but are God's worked examples to show people how they can be sure that they are joined with Jesus and part of God's story. The Church, when it is faithful to Scripture, invites people to change their world-view and accept the good news of God's action in the world.

Jesus is Master of the universe; hear His teaching and see what He is doing in people just like you.

Most people begin to rely on Jesus when they have been exposed to Christian teaching for some time – it takes them a while to finally decide to join in. Many experience the beauty of a Christian community and realise they want what those individuals have. Others find help in a small-group setting, where questions can be raised. Some have sensed God's involvement within their family, or even His specific touch of healing.

One of the key ways to understand who Jesus is and how He can relate to you is to read the Gospels. Mark is the shortest and takes just a few hours to read. The Gospels were largely written so that people who were ignorant of Jesus might receive an appropriate introduction. If you ask God to speak to you as you read you will find that all sorts of things become highlighted, and you will be able to see how your life might change if you put your confidence in Jesus. Each Gospel stresses the last week of His earthly life because this was the fulfilment and ending to which His public ministry had pointed. So it is worth spending time reflecting on His death and resurrection and becoming as sure as you can about their significance and why you need Him to forgive your sin and make you right with God.

Eventually you may get to the point where you change your mind about life's priorities and submit to His leadership. You realise that He must set the agenda for your life. As Jesus commands, 'you believe the good news'; not just in your head but in your heart too, as you realise that putting your confidence in Jesus is the best thing you could do. The language to describe this process varies: some speak of converting, others of coming to faith, becoming a Christian or trusting in God. This language reflects the wide number of word pictures in the New Testament. They all mean the same thing: you are deciding to rely on Jesus for life in this world and the world to come.

The way in which this happens varies from believer to believer. For some it happens over a period of time: they come to realise that it is true, even if they can't think of a specific time. For most though, there is a definite point when they are compelled to talk to God about what they have now realised. They know they have offended Him and that they deserve His judgment. They thank Him for sending Jesus to live, die and rise again, providing this offer of new life. They confess their sin and ask Him to forgive them and send His Holy Spirit to dwell within them. Scripture does not prescribe how followers will feel when they decided to rely on Jesus. For some there are floods of tears; others a sense of great joy; for yet more, a feeling of a burden being lifted; and you might even have all three or none at all! God has His way of drawing near to each one of us and He knows what your response will be – you can trust the experience, however great or mild, to Him.

No club tie required

It is worth underlining what joining with Jesus is not about. It is not like joining a club. When I was sixteen I joined the local golf club, which was just a mile away from where I grew up on the outskirts of Newport on the Isle of Wight. I filled in an application form, which was proposed and seconded by friends of the family, and had a half-hour interview with the kindly club secretary. Central to the interview was 'etiquette': 'Golfing attire to be worn at all times, which meant no jeans. Tailored shorts, not football shorts with long socks, but only when it is very hot. No spikes in the clubhouse, and avoid the course on Wednesday afternoons because it is Ladies' Day.' I was also handed a rule book. Despite the 'rules' the whole thing was actually very friendly and I was duly welcomed as a junior member of Newport Golf Club where I remained until I left the island. If joining with Jesus were like joining a club I might imagine a similar interview on 'kingdom etiquette': how can I look the part and keep the rules if I want to stay in? Some forms of Christianity give the impression that faith is about giving mental assent to the right things, and avoiding wrong behaviour, rather than a relationship with a living person.

The evidences of following Jesus mustn't be confused with the substance. Within the Anglican tradition, for example, confirmation may be a mark of a willingness to trust. Within the Baptist tradition, baptism by immersion will be the symbol used. In most churches, regular attendance at the main meetings of the church would be expected. But the key thing is not what ritual you have practised but whether you have repented and trusted. Where is your confidence? In your behaviour, or in the work of Jesus?

The gift of new life is totally unmerited and not dependent on us cleaning up our act. A genuine change of mind means you want to make the necessary changes to your life – not so that you earn your way into God's good books, but as a joyful response to Christ's work on your behalf and His ongoing concern that you know life in all its fullness.

For one guy it meant breaking up with his girlfriend in order to become a believer. She wanted none of his religion, and he knew that following Jesus meant that he had to stop dating her. Another believer knew that repentance meant no longer following his football team because it was a 'god' to him. It will mean different things for different people, depending on where we are putting our confidence. In short, any alternative god has to go because we can never enjoy the life of God if we are two-timing Him with another lover. Repentance becomes a lifestyle as we learn to turn away from what could become our god and instead put our confidence in Jesus. And believers of all ages face this ongoing battle.

If you are a Christian it may be time to assess why you were attracted to Christianity. Was it to be caught up in His life, or was it an insurance policy because you wanted to hedge your bets against death? You wouldn't be unusual if you signed up on false pretences, but the great news is that God is amazingly gracious and accepts us whatever our motives, and spurs us on. I signed up because I was frightened that I would go to hell. This was not a method of invitation Jesus ever used and I had very little understanding of God's eternal purposes and certainly no intention of playing any part in what He was doing. Praise God that He is not picky how we come to Him!

Starting to live your part

We saw in the last chapter that the stage is set for us to play our part on as soon as we join with God. The rest of this book aims to outline how this works out. But there is a crucial dynamic we must get clear before we continue. God sends His own Spirit to dwell within us.

When we trust Jesus and are born again we become different people because the Holy Spirit awakens our spirit and connects us with God. Spend any time at all reading the Bible and you will realise what an awesome thing this is. In the Old Testament we see that God is so holy and other that only certain people could approach Him in very specific ways. If they got this wrong then death was the certain result. This all changed when Jesus came to earth. Jesus is the one who stands in our place and mediates between us and His Father. Through His death on the cross our sin is covered, and God's Spirit – though part of the Godhead – has been sent to provide a link between us and God so that we are not consumed in His presence. God who is all around us, by His Spirit is especially near. Perhaps a story will help make this clear.

There's a joke that itinerant preachers love to tell which can be adapted to work wherever they are preaching. Imagine they are preaching at All Saints' Church. Here's how the joke would go:

A theological student was visiting churches to decide which one should become his first posting.

His first stop was Holy Trinity. When he got there, the church warden immediately picked up a golden telephone. After talking for several minutes he said, 'Thank you, God,' and hung up.

This shocked the young man. He asked the warden what was so special about the golden phone. 'Well, this phone is a direct line to God. And God tells us whether or not a new vicar might work here.'

The would-be vicar asked if he could use the phone to ask God what church he should pick. 'Sure, you can! But it's going to cost you £1,000; calling heaven isn't cheap.'

Being a poor graduate, the fellow didn't have that kind of money, so he moved along.

His next stop was Christchurch. Upon entering, the warden immediately picked up a golden telephone. After talking several minutes, he said, 'Thank you, God,' and hung up.

The would-be vicar said, 'Hey, I've seen those phones before. Can I use yours to call God and ask which church I should serve in?'

The warden said, 'Sure, but it's going to cost you £750. Calling heaven isn't cheap.'

Again, not having that kind of money, the lad left.

His last stop was at All Saints' Church.
Upon his arrival at the church, the warden picked up a golden telephone, talked to God, and said, 'Thanks,' and hung up.
The boy just had to use that phone, so he said, 'Warden, I really need to use that golden telephone so I can call God and ask Him which church I should serve in.
'From Holy Trinity it was going to cost me £1,000. At Christchurch they wanted £750. So how much will it cost me to call heaven from here at All Saints'?
The warden smiled and said, 'Nothing, son. It's a local call.'

It's a clever joke. Churches love the idea that God is especially close to them and yet know that it isn't actually likely. But it also illustrates a powerful point. God is close to you. God is great and distant, overseeing the whole universe, but also present with us – literally a 'local call' away.

Joining with Jesus means that we start to put our confidence in Him. It will take time for us to learn and grow. Our thinking has been so tied into running our story our way – with little thought for what God may be doing – that we may take a while to transfer all our personal freight from our track to God's. What matters at this stage is not that we have necessarily understood and embraced everything in this book so far, but that we are on the road with God and willing to learn from Him.

In practice, of course, you are unlikely to join with Jesus without first having got to know about Him through meeting with people who are already His followers – we will look at that in more detail in Chapter 5. But at the very start of your journey it has to be just you and Jesus. You appreciating the wonder of His life, death and resurrection, and He extending an invitation to join with Him in exploring what He has for you. Below are some possible responses you may have to what we have considered so far.

What about you?

1. This is all very new to me. I am not sure at the moment.
If you find yourself unable to put your confidence in Jesus then no

amount of 'straining' to believe will work. As I have suggested, you need to ask Him to help you and keep reading the Gospels (Matthew, Mark, Luke and John) to discover more about Him. God's Spirit and God's Word provide the combination for your 'faith' or 'belief' to reach the point where you do put your confidence in Jesus. Left to ourselves we will always write our story our way and figure out ways of justifying our choices. We need God to open our eyes and hearts to His way so that we start seeing things clearly again.

Try to find Bible-believing Christians who can help you further. In the UK, The Christian Enquiry Agency[3] is always willing to help if you want to talk with someone anonymous or find a church that believes the Bible where you can find out more. Give it time. Don't rush; things will become clearer.

2. I have been thinking about this for some time, but have never made the step.

You need to ask yourself why. Are you not sure what to do, or are you nervous about what it will mean? Try and isolate why it is that you have done nothing. God is ready and waiting as soon as you are ready to talk with Him. Maybe you are actually at stage one, above? Maybe you just need to find someone to chat with.

Maybe you don't have a clear vision of what the 'new you' would look like. Maybe you are fearful that parts of the 'you' which you like will be changed. Maybe you need to tell God that you are responding to Him right now. What do you need to repent of? What would putting your confidence in Jesus look like for you? Remember, God is not wanting to mess you about. He knows you and loves you and won't overpower you. He's like a lead dancer who will gently lead you through the steps without treading on your toes.

3. I am ready to join with Jesus.

Great. You simply need to talk to God about it. I wouldn't dream of suggesting what you say, but you will want to tell Him about the ways in which you have changed your mind about Jesus and also that you want to change your priorities. Ask Him to fill you with His Spirit, that you may know the new birth He promises and be enabled to learn from

Him how He wants you to live. Tell someone so they can pray for you. Find some Christians who can encourage you. And read on!

4. I am a Christian already, but a little puzzled by the language you have used to describe faith.
There are many ways of talking about the Christian faith, some focused more on the Bible than others. Some seem to presume that it is all about believing the right things and that 'you are OK for eternity'. God is gracious to all who come to Him, but He always intended a far more intimate daily walk with Him, in the way described above, and has great plans for you. Spend some time reflecting on your Christian life. Would you describe it as a 'relationship with God', or more like signing up for a club – you know you are in, but forget about it most days! God wants so much more for you. Read on!

5. You are describing the sort of life I am living.
Great. I hope you will find the recap of 'joining the leading Player' useful. God wants to continue to work in and through you and help you to be a change agent alongside those He places you with – family, work colleagues, friends, acquaintances. Who do you need to share your story with? I hope that together we can develop 'your part in God's story'.

What joining with Jesus means

- It means you are declared righteous in God's sight because of Christ's life, death and resurrection for you. The future judgment that you would have faced at the end of your life has been brought forward and because of Christ you are acquitted.
- It means that God by His Spirit lives in you, making Jesus real in your experience and able to effect real change within you. You are a disciple of Jesus. Modern words for disciple include 'follower', 'apprentice', 'student'. Dallas Willard helpfully describes a disciple as 'someone who is with Jesus trying to become like Jesus'.

Summary

1. The Gospels and the book of Acts describe how people joined with Jesus and provide a model for how we join with Jesus today.
2. Joining with Jesus means understanding who Jesus is as described in the New Testament – the Gospels especially – so that we reach the point where we are prepared to put our confidence in Him for life and eternity.
3. We receive into our lives the Holy Spirit, who will enable us to know Jesus personally and discover our part in God's story.
4. We need to take appropriate action depending on where we are in the process of getting to know Jesus for ourselves.

Action

1. Work out where you are in the options under 'What about you?' and do what you need to do at this stage of your journey.

Consider

1. Why do you think there are so many different ways in which churches describe joining with Jesus?
2. Think of your friends and family. If there are Christians among them, do you know why they joined with Jesus? What about those who are not yet believers; what puts them off?

Notes

1. Throughout the Old Testament there are hints that someone would come who would answer the people's hearts' cry for a leader and a Saviour – a need shared, of course, by humanity as a whole. Jesus has to be seen in the context of the rest of the story. He is the 'new Adam', one who lives perfectly under the rule and reign of God, as Adam should have done. He fulfils God's promise that all nations would be blessed through Abraham, as the message of His life is broadcast worldwide; He is the deliverer of His people, not just from foreign oppressors, but from slavery to their inbuilt bias against God which leads to death; He sits on King David's throne (the revered king within Israel), ruling over a kingdom that will now fill the whole world; He is God's servant in the

way Israel failed to be, declaring God's love to all people from Brazil to Britain, from Bombay to Beijing. If you are not familiar with the Old Testament, these nuances may be lost on you – but believe me, this is a big deal.

2. There is a tension in the Bible between God's calling of individuals and their response. Theologians have disagreed down through the centuries about the measure to which we have true free choice, given that our choices are constrained by our sinful nature which naturally prevents us from choosing what would be good for us, namely relationship with God Himself.
   God takes the initiative and, in Christ, provides all that we need in order to know Him, but I believe that Scripture depicts us with a measure of freedom within our wills – damaged as they are by sin – that enables us to accept or reject God's overtures. It is down to us and God.

3. The Christian Enquiry Agency, 27 Tavistock Square, London WC1H 9HH
   Tel: 020 7387 3659
   www.christianity.org.uk

03
ENTER THE DRAMA

ENTER THE DRAMA

God has a part for you in His dramatic purposes in the world. Don't stand idly in the shadows, unaware of the exciting adventure of God's glorious plan.

I hate being late. But there is one exception: I don't mind being late for a film at the cinema. In fact, I am actually quite pleased when I arrive at the cinema at the scheduled time for the film because I don't like watching the trailers for other 'soon coming' films. My problem with trailers is that they show so much of the film, that it spoils the surprise factor when you come to see it. So I make a quick judgment on whether there is any chance that I might want to see the film, and sit with my eyes closed and my fingers in my ears and hope people behind are too engrossed in the trailer to notice.

But there's a difference between knowing how the film ends and being desperate for a certain type of ending as the story unfolds. Most stories are predictable, and there's an unconscious agreement between writer and reader or viewer that there will be a resolution: the lost is found, the mystery is solved, the criminals are captured, the hero and heroine fall in love. We finish the story with a satisfied sigh.

An Agatha Christie novel where the Belgian detective, Hercule Poirot, gathers the suspects into a room and declares, 'Well it beats me. I haven't the foggiest idea who did it!', would not be popular. A Bond film where Bond languishes on a life support machine shunned by the women he's been with, would make creator, Cubby Broccoli, turn in his grave. Most films do turn out the way you want them to. We watch in order to be entertained and to see things turn out well. So much of life is murky, unfinished and desperately sad, and we don't want to shell out for more of the same at the box office.

We have already seen that the drama we are involved in does turn out well for the Christ follower. We are putting ourselves in the hands of the world's true hero and we become part of something which is way beyond ourselves. God's story is the true drama of life which we were created for. As John Eldredge puts in his excellent book, *Epic*:

What if all the great stories that have ever moved you, brought you joy or tears – what if they are telling you about the 'true' story into which you were born, the Epic into which you have been cast? … It is a story of beauty and intimacy and adventure, a story of danger and loss and heroism and betrayal.[1]

Eldredge then quotes Frederick Buechner's words from *Telling the Truth*[2]:

It is a world of magic and mystery, of deep darkness and flickering starlight. It is a world where terrible things happen and wonderful things too. It is a world where goodness is pitted against evil, love against hate, order against chaos, in a great struggle where often it is hard to be sure who belongs to which side because appearances are endlessly deceptive. Yet for all its confusion and wildness, it is a world where the battle goes ultimately to the good, who live happily ever after, and where in the long run everyone, good and evil alike, becomes known by his true name … That is the fairy tale of the Gospel with, of course, one crucial difference from all other fairy tales which is that the claim made for it is that it is true, that it not only happened once upon a time but has kept on happening ever since and is happening still.

What Eldredge and Buechner are saying is that we become part of a narrative in which we find our true selves and are lifted in our thoughts and aspirations. The God who began the story intervenes in our world and works with us to bring light into the dark places of our lives and communities. The Gospel is the finest of all stories. Someone has come back to life and offers life to those who know Him.

In a sense, of course, we are part of God's story whether we like it or not. God is the ultimate 'reality' with whom we will one day be involved. I can be on a train which I think is heading for London, but if it is bound for Brighton then I will have to face that reality. If human history is heading for a confrontation with God, then my belief that there is no God, or that God won't mind how I live, won't help me. We need to choose to join in with what God is doing by following Jesus.

But there's a difference between being in a drama as a member of the crowd, and being an actor, with a role and lines, on whom aspects of the script hinge. It is this latter idea that is meant by the chapter heading, 'Enter the drama', and we have great encouragement to do so.

New Testament drama

Jesus' last words to His apprentices in the kingdom reminded them of the drama He was calling them to:

> *Then Jesus came to them and said, 'All authority in heaven and on earth has been given to me. Therefore go and make disciples of all nations, baptising them in the name of the Father and of the Son and of the Holy Spirit, and teaching them to obey everything I have commanded you. And surely I am with you always, to the very end of the age.'*
>
> Matt. 28:18–20

You need to be clear about what the drama is:

All authority in heaven and on earth has been given to me
Jesus is the Master of the universe, the true hero of the world, able to accomplish exactly what He wants.

Therefore go and make disciples of all nations
Jesus chooses to use His followers, the apostles (or disciples), to help people know about God so that they too will become His apprentices, learning from Him how to be like Him. This is not just for the Jewish nation – though it started there – but is open to all peoples everywhere, from Jerusalem to John O'Groats.

baptising them in the name of the Father and of the Son and of the Holy Spirit
The apprentices will need the presence of God within them to change and do the work they are called to do. As the apostles immerse them in water, they are to declare that they are immersed in the Triune God!

and teaching them to obey everything I have commanded you

The apostles are to teach these apprentices about what Jesus said about life in the kingdom, so that they too are able to live the kind of life Jesus did, in character and activity. Matthew and the other three Gospels are the written accounts of what Jesus said and did.

And surely I am with you always, to the very end of the age

Jesus was about to ascend to His Father, but His Spirit would be with them, carrying out His work in and through them. The Spirit would be sent on the Day of Pentecost, soon after.

So Luke begins his second book, Acts, with the words: 'In my former book, Theophilus, I wrote about all that Jesus began to do and to teach until the day he was taken up to heaven' (Acts 1:1–2a). The clear implication is that He is still at work.

As we read the book of Acts we find that Jesus' followers do what He commanded. There's a momentum and vitality about the narrative. The Church is born as the Holy Spirit is given to the apostles in Jerusalem. Inspired by His Spirit they continue the work of telling people of the good news of the kingdom. Peter, in the early chapters, and Paul, from chapter 9, are at the forefront. It is certainly a dramatic time – there are some fantastic responses (3,000 rising to 5,000 joined them), and some violent reactions – early preachers are imprisoned and martyred. People respond to the offer of God's rule in their lives and are healed in the name of Jesus, but new Christ followers have to flee for their lives, leaving Jerusalem for surrounding Judea and Samaria and beyond.

We read of Paul's dramatic conversion from Judaism to Christianity and of his role, with co-workers, in taking the message to Jews and non-Jews throughout the Roman Empire. People respond positively as he travels west across the Roman Empire to Cyprus, Pisidian Antioch, Iconium, Lystra, Derbe, Antioch in Syria, Philippi, Thessalonica, Berea, Athens, Corinth and Ephesus. At each place the focus of the apostles' activity is the preaching of the gospel of the kingdom – telling people that Jesus is the Master of the universe and that this changes everything. Indeed, at the very end of Acts, probably in around AD 62–63, this is what we find the apostle Paul doing.

For two whole years Paul stayed there in his own rented house and welcomed all who came to see him. Boldly and without hindrance he preached the kingdom of God and taught about the Lord Jesus Christ.

Acts 28:30

If Acts is the New Testament history book (and it is also much more), the Letters show us the concerns of the apostles, Paul in particular. Writing to local churches and individuals, they too focus on the way in which these new apprentices in Jesus should understand His life and behave accordingly under God's reign.

Paul tells the Christians at Colosse that they have been 'rescued ... from the dominion of darkness and brought ... into the kingdom of the Son he loves' (ie Jesus) (Col. 1:13).

He tells Christians at Philippi that they are 'citizens of heaven' (Phil. 3:20).

The New Testament includes, too, the end of the drama where, as we saw in Chapter 1, Jesus Christ will return to this planet, judge all peoples – separating those who chose not to join Him from those who did – and renew the planet. It is a glorious finale where those who died believing and those who remain at Christ's coming enjoy a new heaven and earth and are given new bodies fitted for all that God has for us. This is summed up towards the end of the book of Revelation: '"There will be no more death or mourning or crying or pain, for the old order of things has passed away." He who was seated on the throne said, "I am making everything new!"' (Rev. 21:4–5).

Drama in God's story today

God's written revelation finished with the book of Revelation. There are no more books to be written, but as we have seen, everything is in place for you as a Christ follower to enter this drama as a major player whose life and words can make a difference. The book of Acts is sometimes known as the Acts of the Apostles, or, as some name it, the 'Acts of the Holy Spirit'. And the Holy Spirit is still alive and working today.

How are you involved?

The drama you are engaged in concerns your interactive relationship with Jesus in everything you are involved with.

1. The actor
You are the actor! You are an apprentice of Jesus, learning how to live your life under God's rule and reign. As you grow in your apprenticeship, you learn more and more how to live and act like He did.

2. The director
You are indwelt by the director, the Holy Spirit, who makes Christ real to you and who works, as you allow Him to, through the means God directs; for example, prayer, study of the Bible, etc (see Chapter 4). He is also working with other actors and in those who don't yet know Him (John 16:1–4). Nothing can happen spiritually without His work, but He wants to work with you. As you 'enter the drama', He promises to be with you.

3. The location
The 'set' is your home, workplace, car, railway carriage, tennis court, kitchen, hospital bed, favourite chair, favourite walk: ie, wherever you happen to be.

4. The script
You are being taught to view the world differently, from God's perspective, as we saw in Chapter 1. You don't see people as people you can use for your own ends but as people who also need to become apprentices of Jesus. So as God guides you, you pray for them, love them and look to speak to them.

5. The action
This is the love and good works which spring from your walk with Christ and understanding of His cause. The action is whatever God leads you to do. Some of the time you will know how God is leading you to act; sometimes you will be surprised at how He used you in the apparently normal and routine. You might have some dramatic

moments as God acts alongside you, accomplishing what you could never do on your own.

6. The battle

There is an enemy who blinds people and keeps them from seeing the truth. As an agent of the kingdom, you help to free people from Satan's grip as you explain what God is doing and can do for them, and how His Spirit gives life.

Daunting?

If this description of entering the drama has left you thinking you'd rather play a role in a silent movie, or watch someone else play a starring role, maybe I need to put your mind at rest.

Every day you get to choose whether to be part of the crowd or to accept your role in the drama. You may have parts of your life where you prefer to be in the crowd: at work, with certain friends, in college. Maybe you will only want to be in the drama when you are with other Christians, at church, in a small group, when they are praying. You may oscillate between the crowd and the leading role, on the same day. These ups and downs are part of growing to be like Christ. His followers had 'bad days' – you will too. But he who never made a mistake never made anything, and if you are conscious of blowing it, be reassured that Jesus is keen to coach you through the difficulty and show you why things went pear shaped.

Not every day will be filled with dramatic moments. You don't have to feel that you are sparking off a revival – just asking that God may fill you daily with His Spirit so that as you go about your daily business, means you are in touch with the Lord of all. Many faithful Christ followers go months and even years without seeing how their life has yielded a dramatic moment. But that doesn't mean that God undervalues what they do. One day they will know what their faithful labour led to.

Remember, you are a citizen of the King; in touch with Him and living for Him wherever He has placed you. You know the mandate: to make Christ followers and see His rule wherever it is not known. You will get to know what this means within your circle of influence as

Christ leads you by His Spirit and you see things you can change in your family, workplace, school or local club so that God's will is done on earth as it is in heaven.

There are as many types of dramatic moment as there are people. The following examples are all true:

- In a long-standing friendship, someone realises the faith of their friend could be theirs too.
- A girl brings a brother to church and he comes to faith.
- A mother prays for her son for years before he meets a Christian guy who leads him to faith.
- A boss tells his colleagues he is praying for the business and it starts to become successful.
- A prison guard is so impressed with the way a believer responds to his persecutors when he is martyred that he commits himself to Christ.
- An international student is attending an English language school in the UK and meets a Christian who helps her learn English and learn about Jesus.
- A young boy in a Muslim country finds an uncle's Bible, reads it, realises it is true and submits to the rule of Jesus. But he has to leave the country when people hear that he trusts Christ because his life is threatened
- A man is on a life-support machine after open heart surgery. His kidney and liver have failed but God intervenes to the astonishment of the medical profession, and his daughter comes back to faith.
- A woman comes back to faith after a narrow escape in a car accident. She dedicates her life to God who leads her to set up an orphanage in South Africa.

Your dramatic involvement will be different. God deals with each of us differently and there is no formula to follow. I can't guarantee that you will see the same results if your situation is similar to any of the above but I do know that you can involve God in your life in the same way.

Here are some questions to help you 'enter the drama'.

Entering the drama

1. As the actor

Look at your average month (looking at an average week is too short a time frame).

- How much of the time is currently committed to God's story? Be honest.
- Are there areas where you have struggled to involve God?
- How could you change this? When will you change this by?

2. Led by the director

- Do you look to the director (the Holy Spirit) to help you each day?
- Have you received particular direction from Him? (Read Chapter 8.)
- Is there someone who isn't a Christian whom you sense the director might be working in?

3. Using every location

- What resources do you have that can help you communicate the love of God?
- List books such as testimonies and explanations of Christianity, and also CDs and DVDs. (See p.70.)
- Do you think resources could help any of your friends and family?

NB. This is not time for guilt trips. Friends and family may be under our nose, but for various reasons we may be the last person suitable to be of help – they may need a different voice, expressing faith in a different way.

4. Understanding the script

- List the people you know well. How many do you pray for

regularly? Do they relate to God? If you don't know, how could you find out?

- How ready are you to explain to a friend what God has done in your life? Could you do it now? What would you say?
- Talking about God should be the most natural thing. What makes it hard for you?
- What aspects of your faith are you uneasy about? Determine to get some insights into this. (Books listed at the end of this chapter may help.)

5. Engaging in action

- Are there things you could do that would help you get to know friends and relatives better?
- How about arranging something to invite people to: a party, an evening meal, a day at a fun park or a sporting event? Or something longer: a skiing holiday, a summer holiday or booking a large cottage and inviting people to stay.
- What is there at church for people who are not yet Christ followers? Are there categories of people that are missed out? Could you do something for those people?
- Could you lead someone to faith in Jesus?
- How could you learn to lead people to Christ?
- Would you be prepared to pray for someone who isn't a believer?

6. Aware of the battle

- Have you been aware of any particular difficulty in talking about your faith? Is there a Christian you could pray with about this?
- Is it clear to you that God is at work in someone by their reaction?
- How can you better engage in the spiritual battle you are facing?

Your acts?

Advice on explaining Christianity to others sounds great in theory but founders when anyone actually tries to engage with the next-door neighbour over the garden wall, or with the colleague on the journey to a conference.

Every Wednesday for three years I went 'door to door' with a team around the streets close to our church in Bournemouth, trying to talk with people about Christianity. Maybe one person actually attended the church as a result. It wasn't a waste of time – only God will know – and maybe we were just lousy at inviting people! But in the UK you have to ask whether door to door or open air work is the best use of time. Would it have been better to have spent the time getting to know people in leisure settings? But friendship evangelism has a problem too. Do I become a person's friend because I want them to become a Christ follower? Isn't that a bit manipulative? And what if they show no interest – do I move on to someone more receptive?

Perhaps the best way is to think in terms of loving everyone who comes across your path. Some will be acquaintances, others will become closer friends. If you love someone according to the Bible you 'want their good' which will mean talking about faith. In some cases it is easy to mention Christianity early on, in other cases it takes months. But as you pray and converse with God about how best to love them, He will show you. And you keep on loving regardless of whether they show interest or not.

But many of us suffer from what Mark Mittelberg, author of *Building a Contagious Church*,[3] calls the law of spiritual entropy, ie we all naturally focus back on ourselves, and writing our story instead of engaging in God's story. We need to make sure we 'stay in the drama'.

Remaining in the drama

1. Live with the end in mind

Spring Harvest – who run an annual conference at two Butlins holiday camps at Easter time – once entitled a series of meetings, 'Deckchairs on the Titanic'. The clever title conveyed the idea that it was pointless moving the deckchairs around when the *SS Titanic* hit the iceberg in 1912 – there were more pressing matters at hand. It aimed to highlight the trivia with which church life is so often engaged.

Likewise, we are wise if we make sure we involve ourselves in the true drama and not one we concoct as 'important' but which misses out on the eternal reality. K.P. Yohannan, President of Gospel for Asia, surveying the small numbers of Christ followers in parts of India, said:

> *My people have watched the English hospitals and schools come and go without any noticeable effect on either our churches or society. If we intend to answer man's greatest problem – his separation from the eternal God – with rice handouts, then we are throwing a drowning man a board instead of helping him out of the water ... A man's stomach has nothing to do with his heart's condition of being a rebel against the holy God. A rich American on Fifth Avenue in New York City or a poor beggar on the streets of Bombay are both rebels against God Almighty, according to the Bible.[4]*

Yohannan is not denying the value of schools and hospitals; indeed, historically Christians have been at the forefront of their advancement. Watching people starve without helping is an indication that we are far from the compassion of Christ. But it is folly to educate the mind and care for the body if the heart remains untouched. We must do both.

This is why the charity, The Message, in Manchester has ensured that its regeneration work in Greater Manchester has maintained a concern to transform hearts and minds as the community is transformed. Realising that inner-city Manchester lacked any Christian presence, The Message called for Christians to move there and live in some of the rundown areas. They now have ten Eden teams at work in the city. Their presence has helped to affect the neighbourhoods for good, even attracting support from the local police and reports in national newspapers. Local house prices have risen and locals have been encouraged to 'have their community back'. But as the organisation work to see the physical signs of the kingdom, as crime and vandalism are reduced, they continue to be strong evangelistically. In fact, Director of The Message, Andy Hawthorne, himself a keen evangelist, wouldn't have it any other way. You can get government grants for community projects, but no one thanks you for telling them they need Jesus.

2. Develop your character

We have seen how easy it is to drift off to good projects that become the enemy of the best. The antidote to this is to stay in character, spending time with God, reading the Bible and praying, so that you live to your calling and not to the self-focus that characterised life writing your own story. You take yourself wherever you go, so it's no good piling off to do something worthy if when you get there you lack God's agenda – you might have been better off staying at home! If you have ever been harangued by a street preacher whose sensitivity seems to be inversely proportionate to his volume, you will know what I mean!

Finding time to focus on God can be very hard. But it is worth remembering that we don't have time problems – we have priority problems. Many's the time I have been apparently chockablock with time pressures until I have the offer of something I really want to do and, miraculously, the time becomes available! So you need to kick firmly into touch any nonsense about having no time to pray, read the Bible and engage in any of the other disciplines. If you have chosen to follow Jesus, you will make it happen. Just as you somehow manage to find time to eat, even when busy, you can find time for God.

3. Avoid pseudo drama

Any film has extras: people in the street, the man who gets out of the taxi before the hero gets in, the couple by the window who are having a coffee as the heroine waits for her lover. You barely notice them because your eyes are on the action. It would be utterly ridiculous if the main action was disrupted by the main characters deciding that the scenarios that were intended to be the wallpaper of the movie were worth following up. The film footage would be cut immediately. But something very similar wastes the energy of Christ followers. People get involved in petty mini-dramas as if this were the main action. So churches spend hours on gatherings that assist a minimum number of people, or no one at all. There is no direction or presumption that they are supposed to be a community of life-changers. They become barely competent to change the colour of the paint in the annexe. Indeed, you get the feeling that there is a mutual agreement not to engage in any drama.

If you are spending time in church gatherings that don't assist the process of building and equipping the body for life change, then stop attending them. Tell yourself enough is enough. Be gentle; if appropriate explain your reasons – maybe others will agree. But life's too short to be engaged in pseudo drama when you have the adventure of the kingdom to be engaged in.

4. Let words and actions talk together

Look at the way that Christ followers engage in drama and you will find that it starts with words. We are fond of the 'actions speak louder than words' saying because many are fed up with well-intentioned platitudes that are not backed by action. In the kingdom, words are the mechanism God uses for His power to be known: His living Word to us which shapes our thinking and understanding, our words asking God that He might intervene, our words to others explaining appropriately and sensitively what we believe. Words and actions go together.

Engaging in the drama will mean you spending time talking to God about the situations you are drawn to where His will is not being done on earth as it is in heaven, as occasions allow, and talking with people about the joy of being part of God's story. It is part of your confidence in Jesus to believe that what you say to Him, often in your head, is being heard by Him and acted on. You may feel little or nothing when you 'speak', and also sometimes find that what you want is not God's plan after all. But as you pray He will prompt you to act.

It is also part of your confidence in Jesus to believe that if you speak to someone about Him it can make a difference to their life. How can your words affect change in someone's spiritual life? They can as God works. The apostle Paul says:

> *How, then, can they call on the one they have not believed in? And how can they believe in the one of whom they have not heard? And how can they hear without someone preaching to them? And how can they preach unless they are sent? As it is written, 'How beautiful*

are the feet of those who bring good news!'
But not all the Israelites accepted the good news. For Isaiah says,
'Lord, who has believed our message?' Consequently, faith comes
from hearing the message, and the message is heard through the
word of Christ.

Rom. 10:14–17

People can be affected for eternity because you were prepared to be involved in God's story. This is a key theme of the unfolding drama of Scripture as, from Genesis to Revelation, God pursues His people. It's a drama worth entering. When are you going to start?

Summary

1. God has a thrilling story He wants you to engage in.
2. After Jesus returned to heaven, Christ followers became focused on seeing God's kingdom come wherever they were.
3. We are called to 'enter the drama' – God calls us to be a part of what He is doing, seeing our lives as actors under His direction, acting out our faith in the spiritual battle wherever He has placed us.
4. But we will be tempted to leave the drama! We need to live with the end in mind, avoid pseudo drama, and let our words do the talking if we are to maximise our involvement in God's story. When we do, we are in for the great adventure God has for us.

Action

1. Look back at the questions in the section headed 'Entering the drama' and fill out your answers.

Consider

1. If you had to choose someone to play the part of you in the drama of your life story, who would it be?

2. If you died today and someone had to give a talk about your contribution to life, what would they say?

3. Are you happy with what they would have to work on?

Recommended Reading

IDEAS FOR BOOKS/DVDS TO PASS ON TO PEOPLE WHO ARE NOT YET PART OF GOD'S STORY:

Hybels, Bill, *The God You are Looking For* (Authentic).
The book is structured to help you slowly build a complete image of God.

John, J. and Walley, Chris, *The Life – A Portrait of Jesus* (Authentic, 2004).
A fresh 'one-stop' book on Jesus, looking at the evidence for Him, at what He did and at how He can affect our lives today.

Warren, Rick, *The Purpose Driven Life* (Zondervan, 2003).
Rick Warren will guide you through a personal 40-day spiritual journey that will transform your answer to life's most important question: What on earth am I here for?

Nooma is a revolutionary product that is changing the way people experience spirituality – a series of short films on DVD with a 32-page discussion guide. They are outstanding – www.nooma.com.

Books to inspire
CLASSIC BIOGRAPHIES
Elliot, Elisabeth, *Through Gates of Splendour* (republished Tyndale, 2005).
The true story of how, in the 1950s, five young men travelled to make contact
with a stone-age tribe deep in the Ecuadorian jungle.

Pullinger, Jackie, *Chasing the Dragon* (Hodder, 2006).
Stories of how a woman accepts God's call and ends up ministering to drug
addicts in Hong Kong's 'Walled City'.

Ten Boom, Corrie, *The Hiding Place* (Hodder, 2004).
This is the true story of an heroic Dutch family's suffering at the hands of the
Nazis during World War II.

Wilkerson, David, *The Cross and the Switchblade* (Zondervan, 2002).
Stories of gang members coming to faith in the ghettos of New York.

MODERN STORIES
Greene, Mark, *Thank God it's Monday* (Scripture Union, 2001).
An advertising executive shares his story of personal witness in a New York
agency and provides sane and witty advice on why your working life is your
ministry.

Stewart, Tracey, *Payne Stewart: The Authorised Biography* (New Ed edition,
HarperCollins, 2001).
A wife tells the story of how the US open-winning golf star found faith and met a
tragic end in a flying accident.

Wilson, Matt, *Eden: Called to the Streets* (Survivor, 2005).
Christians choose to live in run-down areas of Greater Manchester,
transforming communities and seeing churches strengthened and established.

BOOKS TO DEVELOP YOUR 'ENTER THE DRAMA' SKILLS
Bell, Rob, *Velvet Elvis* (Zondervan, 2005).
A provocative look at the Christian faith which gives a new spin to old truth.

Hybels, Bill, *Just Walk Across the Room* (Zondervan, 2006).
A helpful guide to personal evangelism, full of anecdotes from the author's life.

Manley Pippert, Beccy, *Out of the Saltshaker: Evangelism as a Way of Life*
(IVP, 1999).
Terrific wisdom on making friends and sharing your faith naturally. A classic
that has helped thousands.

Schneider, Floyd, *Evangelism for the Faint Hearted* (Touch of Design, 1994).
An inspirational look at how to share your faith through reading a Gospel with friends.

Wright, Tom, *Simply Christian* (SPCK, 2006).
Regarded by many as one of the finest expositions of Christianity around today, somewhat in the mould of C.S. Lewis's classic, *Mere Christianity*.

Notes

1. John Eldredge, *Epic* (Thomas Nelson, 2004).
2. Frederick Buechner, *Telling the Truth* (HarperSanFrancisco, 1977). As quoted in John Eldredge, *Epic*, op. cit.
3. Mark Mittelberg, *Building a Contagious Church* (Zondervan, 2002).
4. K.P. Yohannan, *Revolution in World Missions* (Charisma House, 1995).

04
PLAN FOR CHARACTER CHANGE

PLAN FOR CHARACTER CHANGE

We learn to become the sort of person whom God can trust with His glorious plans: you can't do it without Him and He won't do it without you.

Actor Daniel Day-Lewis goes to extraordinary lengths to prepare for a role. In 1987, Day-Lewis played a Czech doctor in *The Unbearable Lightness of Being* and insisted on learning Czech and remaining in character – even off screen – for the entire eight-month shooting schedule.

Playing the paralysed Christy Brown in *My Left Foot*, for which he won an Academy Award for best actor, Day-Lewis was wheeled around the set in his wheelchair so he could better understand the restrictions of the character he played, even breaking two ribs from the hunched posture he adopted! Then for *The Last of the Mohicans* in 1992 he underwent rigorous weight training and learned to live off the land and forest where his character lived – camping, hunting and fishing. He even carried a musket at all times during filming in order to remain in character.

He is not of course alone in trying to 'get into' a character, but few in the industry go to such extremes. And many are sceptical of the 'method acting' approach that he and some others adopt. Most believe that the beauty of acting is that you don't have to go to such lengths – that's the very point of it.

When you come to faith in Jesus there is no shortage of people with advice on what you need to do to change your character:

- God will do it for you. You just need to look to Him.
- You are saved by God's grace. There's nothing you need to do. You can 'coast' into heaven, with your salvation ticket safely 'purchased' by Jesus.
- You need to grow the correct way (meaning the way their church grows). This may mean a particular spiritual experience or a particular practice such as baptism by immersion or receiving the gift of tongues.

- You need to get into particular practices: Bible study, prayer, witnessing and giving.
- You need to put in massive effort – if Christ died for you, He calls for everything from you.

Which, if any, are correct?

We saw at the end of Chapter 2 that Jesus invites us to a new kind of life. A disciple (or apprentice) of Jesus is someone who is invited to become like Him by spending time with Him. As we count on Him for everything, He brings us more and more into the life of God, teaching us to make choices that champion God and that are for the good of others, in a life that will go beyond our present one into the glorious future He has for us.

We are not accepted into His family on the basis of our ability to clean up our act, any more than my new nephew, Theo, would only be a family member if he was able to change his own nappy! But now that we are part of the family, we look to bear the family likeness – if we trust Jesus for forgiveness of sins, we can trust Him for life too. No, we can't do change without God, but God won't do it for us: if we sit still and do nothing, nothing will happen! Yes, there may be church-based and private activities that are good for us, but they will be totally superficial if they are not related to the inner work that Jesus is looking to do. He wants us to become like Him, not just act like Him. Maybe Daniel Day-Lewis has something to teach us?

How do we change?

When we look at the way Jesus trained His twelve disciples and the way the New Testament focuses on character change, one thing is abundantly clear – change comes from the inside out. That may sound pretty obvious in the context of what we have been considering, but it is by no means well understood within the Church. Much so-called 'discipleship' presumes that willpower by itself can get the job done – 'just do this and you will be OK' (read the Bible, pray, give, witness, etc).

Jesus is careful to point out the folly of those who think that mere willpower or self-control leads to godliness. The group with willpower in spades was the Pharisees, but rather than receiving commendation from Jesus they were rebuked because they failed to deal with their inner life, presuming that outward conformity was sufficient. His condemnation is summed up with glorious frankness in Matthew 23:25–26: 'Woe to you, teachers of the law and Pharisees, you hypocrites! You clean the outside of the cup and dish, but inside they are full of greed and self-indulgence. Blind Pharisee! First clean the inside of the cup and dish, and then the outside also will be clean.' They were faking it and Jesus knew it.

Others thought that mere superficial keeping of the commandments was 'enough' – 'I haven't murdered anyone, or committed adultery or stolen anything!' But Jesus said that on that basis you might as well remove the parts of the body that do wrong things, then you can't sin at all! Just wanting to sin means that you have a problem. Jesus is looking for more than 'never in any trouble'. He is looking for hearts that are poised to do good.

Change of the self

Jesus is looking for us to co-operate with the Spirit's work within our lives so that we become people who naturally do the sort of things that He would do. Yes, willpower is involved; we will need to exert effort, but in co-operation with God as He directs. We need to see our will (also known as spirit or heart) in the context of the other dimensions of the self. When asked which of the commandments were greatest, Jesus replied: 'Love the Lord your God with all your heart and with all your soul and with all your strength and with all your mind'; and, 'Love your neighbour as yourself' (Luke 10:27).

It is not just the heart but all the dimensions of the self that are to be trained in the ways of God. We operate as whole people. I do not dissect my desire for a piece of chocolate into bodily desire, thought, feeling and action! But for the purposes of understanding how the self changes it is handy to look at each in turn.

The dimensions of the self are as follows:

- the mind (thoughts and feelings)

- the heart (the centre of the life where our spirit, or will, is active)
- the soul
- the body

I would stress that there is no 'formula' for growth, least of all in what we are about to look at. God has an individual agenda for each of us. Nevertheless, a basic understanding of how God sees the dimensions of the self is a great base for us to use when looking at character change.

Dimensions of self

1. Thinking
The transformation of the inner life will start with the mind (which comprises thinking and feeling). Jesus wants to teach you how to think. Our thoughts are the ways we are conscious of things, linked closely to our beliefs and our memories. What you think about is your first freedom. The Bible talks of the way in which our foolish minds were darkened before we came to faith. We wrote our old story as best we could, but it was often based on lies. Our belief system had left out the source of truth, which gave us a wonky view of ourselves, our world and God.

It was a thought that first enabled us to join God's story. We heard or read about God's love and the gospel and, as God's Spirit was at work, we received it as truth. It may have taken time, questioning and reflection but eventually we had it clear enough in our minds to take action. Jesus is looking to further transform our thinking so that it is more and more based on God's truth and less and less on the lies we receive daily from the media and those around us: lies about our true value, lies about what life is about, lies about how to be a success in life. He will transform our thinking as we receive His truth through reading the Bible and hearing it taught. As we understand the implications of what it means for Jesus to be Master of the universe and see life through His eyes, we have the foundations for a change in our whole character.

This is why the apostle Paul wrote that we are to be transformed by the renewing of our minds (Rom. 12:2). We start to understand that God is good, that the world is a great place to be and that God has wonderful plans for us. We see ourselves as we should – as image-bearers with a great destiny in God – as we learn how to live with Him and receive His grace.

In particular, as those seeking to become like Jesus, we are especially concerned to note what Jesus is like. If we have a vague or muddled idea of Jesus, it is unlikely that we will actually want to be like Him, however good the notion may sound. The four Gospels give us a clear picture of why Jesus is so attractive in His earthly life:

- His love for fellow men and women
- a generosity of spirit to everyone, irrespective of background
- an outgoing nature
- you can take Him at His word
- He cares for the downtrodden and downcast
- He is totally relaxed and cool, with an accepting spirit, even at His time of turmoil prior to the cross
- He is great fun at parties: people want Him there – even if what He says and the stories He tells sometimes make listeners uncomfortable
- a joyful spirit – glad to be alive and enjoy His Father's creation (which He, in His pre-incarnate state, helped to build) John 1:3; Col. 1:16
- He is welcoming to children (unusual at the time) and has a great rapport with women, who clearly adore Him (Luke 8:1–3), yet doesn't relate to them in ways that would make them uncomfortable
- He stands up for what is right, spots hypocrisy and abuse of power and speaks against those responsible
- He is never vindictive or malicious and wants the best for those He meets and knows about

What governs your thinking when you have a quiet moment?

What is your greatest source of fuel for thinking? Family? Friends? TV? Books? Bible?

2. Feelings

It has been well said that feelings are great servants but lousy masters. Our modern age lives by the slogan, 'If it feels good, do it'. We ask people how they feel, not how they think. Feelings govern our lives. If we don't feel like shopping, we don't do it unless we have to (or are dragged there by our partner). But feelings are deceptive: they make us want to do things we know are not correct and they can change so fast that we don't know where we are and what we 'feel'. If we only based our living on how we felt, we would get into a lot of trouble! And of course many do.

As you grew up, your feelings played a large role as your inner world was formed. Maybe you gave in to your feelings of anger, of lust, for food or to look good, and reaped the consequences? And, of course, some of your feelings stemmed from a wrong view of God, yourself and the world. You were like a survivor of a plane crash stuck in the middle of the desert but with the wrong map.

Jesus is aiming to transform your feelings so that they become part of the positive transformation of character and not a handicap. As we have already noted, it is not a simple matter of telling them to 'get in line'. They are too complex and powerful within us for us to simply will change. Have you never felt something for someone you didn't want to feel (for good or ill)? Could you simply flick an emotional switch?

It is easy to oversimplify at this point but essentially feelings will change as we think correctly about life in God. We will be able to recognise those feelings that are destructive and seek to cultivate those that are in keeping with the heart of God. In the short term you learn to do what is right regardless, realising that you do not need to give in to your feelings and that you will not 'die' if you don't get what you want, in the way you want it. But as you overcome destructive feelings you will know that you need to work with Jesus so that they are replaced with feelings from the heart of God. These will include chiefly love, joy and peace; the first three of the spiritual fruit which God is developing in you: 'love, joy peace, patience, kindness, goodness, faithfulness, gentleness and self-control' (Gal. 5:22–24). Love is willing the good of another, joy, is a pervasive sense of well-being, and peace is a settled assurance of how things will turn out. As you see life as God sees it and respond in trust, these qualities will start to grow.

We need to be very discerning when handling our feelings. They are like the warning light on a car's dashboard showing that something is wrong. But be careful. In some cases your feelings may be a symptom of something that has nothing to do with the inner life – you are tired, hungry or in physical pain. And in some cases you may need specialist help from a trained counsellor to understand what you are feeling and why, or simply just a friend to talk things through with.

Do you have dominant feelings you know need to change?

3. Heart

It is only after considering thoughts and feelings that we come to our heart (also spirit and will). This is the core of who we are. We are defined by the choices we make: our consents and non-consents which form our character. And it is here that we are perhaps most aware of the distance between what we want and what Jesus wants. We may have accepted that Jesus is the Master of the universe, but that doesn't mean we are yet at the point where our will has become His. Yes, He reigns, but we still want to rule our kingdom our way!

Your capacity to choose God and follow Jesus will be a result of how you think about Him, what you know He wants of you, how you feel about that, and whether your body is in line to function appropriately. But the will also has a place within your internal loop. As you choose your thoughts, and hence your feelings, and choose how to manage your body (we will look at this later in this chapter) you are better able to choose to follow Jesus. Indeed, it will come 'naturally' to you – you will find that you don't want to do anything else. So, if your spare thinking time is spent watching X-rated movies, listening to punk rock music, reading horror fiction and never reading Scripture, you will not know what Jesus calls you to do and certainly won't do it.

Why do many make little progress in their Christian life? The answer is simple and staring at them: they don't want to! They know they should want to, they know it makes sense, but when they read about Jesus and His teaching they prefer life as it is. We need to get to the point where we want to want to change; where we say, 'OK, at the moment I don't want to give up X but if Jesus says X needs to go, I am willing to learn from Him so that I get to the point where I want it to go too. I am determined to change.' Jesus wants you to get to the point where your will is so close to His that He can empower you to do what you want. It's a staggering thought, but it won't happen overnight.

Do you want to be like Jesus? Do you want to want to?

4. Body

The body is often overlooked when it comes to character development. After all, it is the inner life that is being considered. But we are whole people and live from our bodies and, in truth, our body takes on the quality of the inner self – when you are overtaken with grief or rage or lust, your whole body is engaged in the emotion. The body is linked intricately with the rest of the self and it was intended by God to be a blessing. The fact that God became human in Jesus is proof that it is essentially good, even though, Jesus apart, it can be the vehicle for much evil. It is through the body that the inner self is known to the outside world, and it is our body that displays character and through which we fake character.

Our bodies are part of an internal feedback loop, which operates as regularly as a machine. Indeed, in extreme cases such as addictions, people will say they cannot help their behaviour. The truth is, more people are addicted to bodily actions than we realise. Hence those words of Jesus, 'the spirit is willing but the flesh is weak'.

In your life story written without God, your thinking and feelings have led your body to seek your good. It was more often poised to do evil rather than good. I don't mean that you were prone to habitual shoplifting, but living in the self-focused way many live: cursing rather than blessing, worrying rather than praying, lusting rather than loving, grasping rather than relaxing, arguing with malice rather than reasoning with grace. The idea of loving God with your whole being and loving (wanting the good of) your neighbour as yourself was beyond you. But as the Word of God and the Spirit of God do their work, our bodies can learn to be ready to do good, as we will note later in this chapter.

Is your body mainly a help or a hindrance when it comes to character change?

5. Soul

The soul is perhaps the most slippery of the parts of the self to describe, partly because it is hidden within the depths of the self. Dallas Willard says: 'the soul is that aspect of your whole being that correlates, integrates and enlivens everything going on in the various dimensions of the self. It regulates whatever is occurring in each dimension and how it interacts with the others. The soul is "deep" in the sense of being foundational and also in the sense that it lies almost totally beyond conscious awareness.'[1]

The soul has been described as functioning in our life like the hard drive in a computer, working in the background as our life carries on. Or perhaps like the central heating system in a large office which keeps the temperature pleasant and is only noticed when it goes wrong. Most people barely know and recognise the soul, not least because some have concluded that it doesn't exist. But it is a vital part of who we are. It is spiritual in nature and, as Willard explains, serves to link the parts of the self together. When God acts to liberate the spirit, the soul too is brought alive to God.

How do you think of your soul, if at all? Have the images in this section helped?

Transforming your inner world

Having these dimensions of the self (thinking, feeling, body, soul and heart (will/spirit)), and noting that they interact and intersect within us as we live, we are ready to see the self transformed so that we take on the character of Jesus – we become like Him.

We have noted the way in which God's Spirit works to give life to our spirit as we hear and respond to God's Word and, principally, the news of Jesus. But we need to know how we further co-operate with God for transformation to take place.

It is often assumed that because Jesus is God, He didn't need to nurture His inner life during His time on earth. But throughout His life we see that He did just that. Indeed, His followers asked Him to teach them to pray because they realised this was an aspect of His life with God which they needed to learn. If there were practices that Jesus used then you can be sure that we will need to do the same.

This highlights a principle that we need to be clear on which can transform our outlook on character growth: direct effort will not enable you to become like Jesus. But there are things you can do indirectly which will help you to.

Let me illustrate. When I was a student at Wye College, London University near Ashford, Kent in 1981, I attended the Christian Union (known as the CF). The college is now run by the University of Kent in association with Imperial College, London, but then it was one of the foremost colleges of agriculture and related subjects – I studied agricultural economics. There were people in the CF that were delightful – the kind anyone would warm to. But there were two guys in particular to whom I took a dislike. I didn't know why, and no one else seemed to object to them. There was just something about them that wound me up. When I went to a meeting and they were there, the meeting, for me, was spoiled and after a while I knew there was a problem I had to deal with. I knew that one of the primary ways in which people see Christianity being real is when Christians love one another. I knew I was letting the side down – I was beginning to really hate these guys! I knew that love is an action, not just an emotion – it is 'seeking the good will of another', but neither action nor emotion was within my grasp.

I wish I had known this principle then because no amount of trying to love really worked. The more I tried, the harder it got, until I came across a book that encouraged me to pray for people I didn't get on with, however hard it seemed. So I did. I put them on a daily prayer list I used in those days and, bit by bit, I started to feel differently and act differently, so that by the end of the first term the problem had disappeared. I was unwittingly practising this principle. By direct effort I could not be like Jesus but I could do something (pray) which indirectly enabled me to be like Jesus.

By willpower we cannot do the things Jesus calls us to do: take a look at the 180 or so commands in the Gospels. We cannot love, we cannot forgive, we cannot bless others when they curse us, we cannot abandon lustful thoughts, or stop gossiping, and mean it. We can fake it, of course. Willpower will give us the appearance of good behaviour, rather like the Pharisees, but Jesus had to warn them that their hearts were far from God. In truth, willpower has no power.

But there are activities that Jesus practised and that we can practise which will enable us to change. They enable us to better co-operate with what God, by His Spirit, is looking to do. They have been a source of strength and help to God's people throughout the centuries, even if some are neglected in modern Christianity. It is worth stressing that the activities do not give us merit before God. This is not 'Gold-standard Christianity' for those who pay higher premiums. But they are activities within our power which enable us to do other things not within our power, as God is able to work. For example, I couldn't naturally love those guys in the CF, but prayer enabled God to work in me so that I could love them.

There are many lists of these types of activity. Perhaps the best known are the ones listed in Richard Foster's book, *Celebration of Discipline*,[2] which are divided into three categories:

The inward disciplines

MEDITATION: mulling over the Word of God, often involving memorising key parts

PRAYER: conversation with God about our life together

FASTING: the giving up of something – normally food – so that we can more easily focus on and receive from God

STUDY: concerted time focusing on the Bible and books about the Bible so that we better understand what is being said

The outward disciplines

SIMPLICITY: paring life down to the bare essentials by getting rid of clutter and excess

SOLITUDE: spending significant periods alone (I suggest one hour minimum) and in silence so that we can catch up with ourselves and God

SUBMISSION: laying down the burden of needing to get our own way; being willing to accept others' authority or choices, especially God's

SERVICE: willingly working for others, often in secret, knowing that it is God whom we ultimately serve

The corporate disciplines

CONFESSION: expressing our sins and failings to God and, where necessary, to others

WORSHIP: the conscious living of all of life in praise to God, including praise in word and song with other Christians

GUIDANCE: seeking God's help as we live our life, listening to the voice of His Spirit and counsel from His people

CELEBRATION: the enjoyment of God and life in play and laughter, dancing and food, according to the preferences of the group we are with

Some of these practices, such as prayer, study and worship, form the backbone of the life of most churches. Others, such as solitude, silence and fasting, are less practised, depending on the church tradition, though many regard them as just as vital.

It is clear that most of these practices are bodily acts. After all, where else would we live but in the body? But they are disciplines that enable the different parts of the self to be transformed. If you want four to start with, then solitude and silence, study and worship are good ones to go for. As we spend time in solitude and silence for significant periods, not focusing on anything in particular, the 'revs' in our life begin to calm down, we start to feel less harassed and more centred on God, and we are able to interact better with Him. If you are 'typical' of most people, you will probably need to find a quiet place for this, and maybe spend time with God early in the morning or late at night.

Study and worship help us to focus our thinking on God. You need to study for an extended amount of time – at least thirty minutes at a stretch. You could memorise verses or, better still, passages, so that your mind can turn to them when you need them (Psa. 119:11). Worship is the expressing of worth to God – in prayer privately and corporately – as we sing words others have composed for us. The two go together – study without worship increases head knowledge but not relationship; worship without study means we lack any focus and content to our praise.

Taking just these four disciplines, you can see how your thinking can become Godward as you reflect on your life in Jesus and appreciate what He intends for you. Your feelings will gradually change to come into line with your thoughts and as, through solitude and silence, you become less dependent on the surrounding world, your response to people and situations become more centred on God. Thus, the soul, which cannot be accessed directly, becomes more at peace as the dimensions of the self become focused on God.

Through these practices God is able to work and do great things in you. You start to have the resources in place to do the things Jesus calls you to do such as love your enemies, bless those who curse you. You are able, as Paul says, to 'put on Christ'. You become someone who is naturally producing the fruit of the Spirit within your life: love, joy, peace, patience, kindness, goodness, faithfulness, gentleness and self-control.

Jesus is looking forward to you learning from Him how to better handle whatever situation you may find yourself in. For example, if you find commuting unpleasant, are struggling to find work, or have the burden of care for an elderly relative, that will be the place of training. You don't have to go anywhere. He's with you now. It's just a case of learning to see what you used to see within your story, through God's eyes.

Those who think there is nothing we can do to make ourselves become more like Jesus until we get to heaven are dead wrong. They are in danger of missing out on the training that Jesus provides in this life which has some bearing on what happens in the next.

Those who think that God will help them change are partly correct but fail to realise that it does require effort from them; God will not do it for them. They are correct in believing that it is the grace of God that is vital (God acting to do what they cannot do themselves) but fail to realise that effort is still required. This effort is not earning their salvation, but obeying God in what He is calling them to do.

And those who think it is all about willpower are correct to say that effort is required, but wrong to think that we can affect the changes required by direct effort. Method acting works for Daniel Day-Lewis, but only needs to work for as long as he is playing the role. The changes that God intends are true character change that will last for eternity.

You may be wondering, why all this talk of character? Why haven't we focused on being fitted for the role in God's story that God has for you? Isn't living in the kingdom about a new kind of power, seeing God's intervention in our murky and dark world as part of His cosmic plan for renovation and restoration of all things?

As we shall see in later chapters, God is indeed planning for you to be prepared for a front-line role, but He is keen to work on character first. Jesus, prior to His crucifixion, met with His followers in Jerusalem for one last time and reminded them to stay close to Him, for unless they did they could do nothing.

Just as a wise parent will gradually take away restrictions for children so that they can start to choose for themselves, so God gives us the freedom to grow. He is not in your face when you wake up. There is no automatic feeling of dread that engulfs you when you leave home without reading your Bible. You will not be forced like an involuntary puppet to speak of your faith in company. He is giving you freedom to grow. You control the pace (to a certain extent) and when you are ready He will trust you with active participation in what He is doing.

He's got a long-term plan for you and me that He's looking forward to carrying out, and there will be more than enough power and fireworks when we are ready. But He first needs you to 'plan for character change'. Will you?

Summary

1.   There is a lot of confusion among Christians about how and whether change takes place.
2.   Change is firmly on the agenda for the apprentice of Jesus and it's good news.
3.   The change Jesus has in mind is change in the inner life: thoughts, feelings, body, soul, heart (will/spirit).
4.   We cannot change the inner life by direct effort.
5.   We co-operate with God by practising activities that enable Him to develop the inner life.
6.   This character change is the basis of the new kind of life Jesus brings.

Action

1. Look back through this chapter. What do you need to incorporate into your life?
   For example, a regular time for reading the Bible and praying; times of solitude, maybe taking a half or full day if circumstances allow; being more regular at worship services.
2. Ask God to use this chapter and your response to develop your character.

Consider

1. Why is character change so hard?
2. Have you sought character change and failed? Are there things in this chapter that could help you?

Notes
1. Dallas Willard with Don Simpson, *Revolution of Character* (Navpress, 2005).
2. Richard Foster, *Celebration of Discipline* (Hodder & Stoughton, 1980).

Further Reading
Foster, Richard, *Celebration of Discipline* (Hodder & Stoughton, 1980).

Peck, Andy, *Coached by Christ* (CWR, 2005). This book contains fuller chapters on the dimensions of the self.

Willard, Dallas, *Spirit of the Disciplines* (HarperCollins, 1990).

Willard, Dallas with Simpson, Don, *Revolution of Character* (Navpress, 2005).
This is a simplified version of *Renovation of the Heart*, Dallas Willard (IVP, 2004), which is also highly recommended.

05

LINK WITH CO-STARS

LINK WITH CO-STARS

You can discover your part in God's story when you team up with people who are also on track with God. Your ability to find your part will depend to some degree on who you link with.

Remember the story you heard at school about the tortoise and the hare? They argue about who is faster and decide to settle the argument with a race. The hare is ahead but gets complacent, sits under a tree and falls asleep. The tortoise keeps going and wins the race. The moral of the story is given as: 'slow and steady wins the race.' And that's how most people leave it.

But apparently the story doesn't end there. The hare realises why he has lost and demands a re-match, and this time he wins by several miles. Then the tortoise, bruised by the second encounter, outsmarts the hare by choosing a new course for a third race which includes crossing a river. His ability to swim on the watery part of the course renders the hare's speed irrelevant. This time the tortoise wins and now the moral is rather different: 'first identify your strength and then change the playing field to suit it!'

But there is a final twist. The hare and the tortoise by this time have become pretty good friends and do some thinking together. Both realise that the last race could have been run much better. So they decide to do the last race again, but to run as a team this time. They start off, and this time the hare carries the tortoise until the river bank. There the tortoise takes over and swims across with the hare on his back. On the opposite bank the hare again carries the tortoise and they reach the finishing line together. They both feel a greater sense of satisfaction than they'd felt earlier. The hare and the tortoise learn another vital lesson. 'When we stop competing against a rival and instead start competing against the situation, we perform far better.'

In this final version of the story, the hare and the tortoise make a good illustration of how those who are writing God's story might act. You and I will perform better when we work with others and don't compete with them. We need each other to fulfil what God has placed within us. Our part in God's story will be alongside others, working with them, using our gifts and energy to accomplish collectively what we couldn't alone.

The Bible demonstrates this interplay between individuals and community as God calls first a family (The Abrahams) who become tribes (of Israel) who become a nation at Sinai on the way to their new home (Canaan).

In the New Testament Jesus quite deliberately chooses twelve disciples (mirroring the tribes) and these disciples go on to establish communities based around the kingdom of God, after Jesus has returned to heaven.

When you become part of the kingdom you are by definition part of 'the Church' that exists worldwide. The word 'church' is a translation of a Greek word meaning 'assembly', which the early Christians used to describe those 'called out ones', ie those who are under God's rule and reign and thus believers in Jesus. A Christian is therefore part of the universal Church who then joins with a local community of believers.

In *Resident Aliens* Stanley Hauerwas and William H. Willimon put the concept of joining the cast like this: 'The story began without us, as a story of the peculiar way God is redeeming the world, a story that invites us to come forth and be saved by sharing in the work of a new people whom God has created in Israel and Jesus. Such movement saves us by:

1. placing us within an adventure that is nothing less than God's purpose for the whole world;
2. communally training us to fashion our lives according to what is true rather than what is false.[1]

It may be that you are already linked in with a local church, or are at the stage where you need to find one. Since I believe that the perspective of this book is literally life changing, I am keen that you are nurtured in joining in God's story by people who share a kingdom-focused perspective. What should you look for in a church and what happens if you don't find it?

What to look for

The ideal environment that I am going to describe may exist in a local church, or in a part of that church: a small group or cell group with fewer numbers. If you have had to move around a lot, it may be that members of your previous churches, or friends, provide the ideal in the way that your weekly church cannot. The ideal I describe will focus specifically on how the community helps you in staying linked to God's story. As such, it makes no mention of size of church, denomination, styles of worship, practice of the sacraments or church government; all of which are important, but not especially pertinent to our discussion here.

1. Kingdom vision

Back in the 1990s there was a craze involving Magic Eye pictures. These were pictures which to the casual observer seemed to merely depict weird shapes and colours. However, if you mastered the knack of focusing and then relaxing the eye, you could view the most glorious 3-D picture. Preachers have noted the parallels between this and a sudden realisation about God and spiritual life. But this can also apply to a vision for the way people can live. You want to link with Christians who share your vision for God's kingdom. They may articulate it in a different way, but you know that the bottom line is that they want to see God's reign and rule known in as many people as possible. When they look at the world and their potential under God they see what you see.

The kingdom vision may be articulated by the church leaders or pastor, but also needs to be embodied by the lives of those who lead. You need to be able to see what following Jesus looks like in your inner-city neighbourhood, rural village, estate or suburb.

The vision leads naturally to values. If your desire is that the world may be impacted by Christians, then the way the church community is arranged should facilitate this: they should acknowledge that people's roles in the family, workplace and at leisure can provide kingdom moments and so this is time to be nurtured and valued.

It is astonishing how the 'values temperature' can vary from one Christian community to another. In a former life I used to visit university Christian Unions as a student worker. At one CU I attended a prayer meeting and discovered just a handful had come from a total of eighty members.

'Where is everyone?' I asked.

'Oh this is normal,' said one of the attenders. 'Not many show up for the prayer meeting.'

I travelled just forty miles to another CU later in the week. I attended their prayer meeting too. They were sad that only 110 out of the 200 members were there.

'Really disappointed with the numbers,' said the prayer secretary, slightly embarrassed that the 'poor' attendance should be when I was there!

The two CUs had exactly the same types of student. There was no difference other than their numbers. But one was convinced few would come, the other expected more. One CU put a high value on prayer, the other didn't.

In the same way, church communities can have a massively different perspective. In one church in China, a believer who doesn't see people coming to faith faces discipline by the church! (I should add that the discipline is in the form of training by an older Christian who helps them with personal witness.) In many churches in the UK, years will go by without anyone coming to faith and no one bats an eyelid!

I recently had the privilege of visiting the headquarters of The Message – a charity that aims to give the young people of Manchester the opportunity to hear the gospel repeatedly. Every week the 100-plus full-time workers and volunteers come together to pray and worship and every month spend a day in prayer, sharing stories so that the kingdom vision remains strong.

2. Shared strategy

Venus and Serena Williams have a dad who is passionate about their success. It began when Richard Williams watched the women's tennis champion receive her prize at the 1978 French Open on TV. There and then he determined that if he had any more children, they would become tennis players. So when Venus was born in 1980 and Serena in 1981, he eagerly awaited the day when they could hold a tennis racket. Taught from the age of four, the sisters dominated the tennis scene in southern California, and were both number one in their age categories. But instead of leaving them to compete within the juniors circuit, Williams moved the whole family across the US to Florida, to a top tennis academy, for four years.

It was in the company of others who were training specifically for tennis stardom that the sisters' careers received their foundation. In September 1999, the seventeen-year-old Serena defeated Martina Hingis in the finals of the US Open, becoming the first African-American woman to capture a Grand Slam singles title since the late 1950s. In 2000, Venus began a winning streak that took her all the way to Wimbledon, where she grabbed a Grand Slam title of her own, beating defending champion, Lindsay Davenport, in the finals and making some history of her own. Just one day later, Venus and Serena teamed up to win the Wimbledon doubles title. For Richard Williams it was definitely a case of mission accomplished.

Looking back on their development, there is no doubt that if they had stayed in southern California they would have found it much harder to reach their potential. There is no doubt too that it was their father's strategy that helped them.

We have our mission statement from Jesus, but need the work of the Spirit in community with others for us to decide how we might put this into practice in our neighbourhood. Your impact on the community will be greater if you work with your friends on a shared strategy. Imagine that you invite someone to a church meeting. Your friends will be stronger in some areas than you. You may be great at inviting the person, someone else great at welcoming and someone else at articulating the gospel. Furthermore, you represent just one personality that is becoming like Christ. Your 'co-stars' will bring their personalities to the task and may well relate to your friend better than you. Being within a community that has a shared strategy can provide enormous impetus, particularly if seasons of life make focus on what God is doing especially hard.

3. Real interaction
It was the evangelical statesman and Rector Emeritus of All Souls,

Langham Place, London, John Stott, who said that the church should have the same sort of characteristics as a good pub when it comes to providing an environment where people can relate. In fact, the signature song of a sit-com set in a pub, albeit an American-style bar, *Cheers*, expresses the aspirations of the New Testament church rather well:

> *Sometimes you want to go where everybody knows your name and they're always glad you came, you want to be where people can see your troubles are all the same, you want to be where everybody knows your name.*

You want to go: this is not an obligation – 'OK, I ought to attend church' – rather it's a pleasure.

Where everybody knows your name: maybe not everyone, but enough for you to feel welcome.

They are always glad you came: the church, when it is at its best, values all who come, regardless of race, colour, intellect, cultural background.

Our troubles are all the same: we are all infected by the sin virus, have been rescued by Jesus and are battling to remove the effects of the pollutant so that God's image within us shines through.

In such an environment there are people who can help me spot where sin has a grip, and graciously help me to 'change my mind' about it and see the grace of God work more powerfully. I need people to remind me that God is at work within me to want good things, and that my potential in Him is extraordinary.

4. Helpful feedback

In the film, *Crocodile Dundee*, Paul Hogan, who plays the brash outback Aussie character, says that in his community, problems are easily solved. To paraphrase the comment: 'If I have a problem. I tell my mate Walt. He tells everybody. End of problem!'

This may work for the outback of Australia but it's actually supposed to be rather different in church. As we learn from Jesus how to become like Him, our human interactions will change. We learn to love God, but we are also learning to love our neighbour. But learning how to do this takes time. I may want things to go well with my neighbour, but may not always be sure what is best, or know how my attempts are being received. I will need to receive feedback on how I am doing from people I trust, who can gently explain what's going well and what isn't. If you have a problem with Betty, Bert, Mavis and Malcolm, then someone probably needs to tell you that 'you are the problem'!

Church at its best includes the receiving of biblical instruction as we interact with one another. We should try and note, within our reactions, the ways in which we fall short of the desire to love our neighbour as ourselves. This can only properly happen in a setting with people who truly know us. It may be a formal small group, or with other Christians we know and trust whom we can meet up with from time to time.

I am not pretending that giving or receiving feedback about personal lives is easy. But this is one of God's ways of helping us grow. Marriage is obviously a great place for two people to learn at close quarters how their natural way of relating can wind up another person. Good friendships, where trust has been established and where we know the friend wants our good, will also provide a growth environment.

What you may find

The ditty goes like this: 'to dwell above with saints we love, that will be glory. To dwell below with saints we know, that's quite another story.'

Or as a good friend once noted: 'The Bible says it is a fearful thing to fall into the hands of the living God, but it isn't much fun to fall into the hands of God's people!'

Just as you and I are not the finished article, so local churches have their share of ups and downs because they are not the finished article either.

The content of this book will be a challenge for some churches. Here's why:

- Some churches are dominated by leaders who do not have a kingdom mentality. They seem more concerned with their own agenda than God's.

- Some church leaders are not keen on equipping people to live their story because they want their own ministry to flourish. They focus their energy on what happens in church gatherings and make little attempt to empower people to see their lives as having equal value in the eyes of God, and equal potential in the kingdom.

- Some churches have effectively opted to live out an edited version of God's story. They have selected the parts they like and discarded the rest. For example, they may stress the legalistic side and leave out grace, or misunderstand the grace side and not see their role in the world.

Consequently, many church communities pay lip service to learning to follow Jesus within the kingdom. It is just not on the agenda and not likely to be. Playing church occupies their whole time instead!

What if your church does not share your vision of the kingdom?

1. Remember we are all flawed

Those who say that we need to get back to the New Testament church forget some of the original characteristics. Specific situations included: jealousy over food distribution (Acts 6), stand-up rows over table manners (Gal. 2), incest (1 Cor. 5), name calling (1 Cor. 1), gossip, major disagreement (Phil. 4), treachery (Alexander in 2 Tim. 4:14), heretical teaching (Jude 4), attempts to dominate (3 John 9–10). And that's not to mention the many areas which the apostles warned about in their letters, some of which would have been genuine problems (Col. 3:5–10).

The cliché, 'You'll never find a perfect church and if you do don't join', is ever true! You don't want to become like some Bible teachers, so individualised in what they like and don't like. So don't expect everything to be perfect!

2. Share your vision wisely

Jesus tells us not to put pearls before swine (Matt. 7:6). Some interpret Jesus' words as meaning we should leave fools to their own devices: if they don't see the glorious future they can have in Christ, then leave them to their small-minded lives! In fact, the metaphor is rather more obvious. Pearls cannot be digested by swine who are just looking for a piece of husk to chew on. You and I would welcome pearls but to swine they are as much use as a bag of nails.

In the same way the ideas in this book, encouraging someone to play the glorious part they can have in God's story, may not be digestible. You need a strategy which offers them more digestible ideas bit by bit. So it is worth asking questions. You might be able to spark something off that helps them switch from being an extra to a co-star.

- Be clear that it is the Word of God that gives you confidence.
- Be humble about what God may be doing through you. Don't presume that you have a 'hotline to heaven' even if you are pretty sure that you know what God is doing.
- Be confident about God's commitment to that person, and His willingness to work with them to accomplish great things.

3. Seek to understand

Stephen Covey's book, *The Seven Habits of Highly Effective People*[2] lists as one of the habits: 'seek first to understand before you seek to be understood.' It was Abraham Lincoln who said, 'When I get ready to reason with a man, I spend one third of my time thinking about myself and what I am going to say – and two thirds thinking about him and what he is going to say.' But it is possible to do that and still not actually listen! We use the time when someone speaks as thinking time to prepare what we are going to say, instead of really thinking and understanding. As James puts it, 'Everyone should be quick to listen, slow to speak, and slow to become angry' (James 1:19).

It is important to try and understand why the Church is the way it is. Some churches have consciously rejected attempting to live God's story, others have never quite grasped it, maybe because of inadequate Bible teaching. Both situations are sad, but it is helpful to sense where the problem lies. If a church actively rejects a kingdom approach you may be less inclined to think there could be a change, than if it is down to ignorance.

4. Confront issues
As carefully as possible, you might want to talk to people about what they believe and why they believe it. Even when people apparently share the same vision, relational harmony may be some way off. Scripture abounds with examples of apparently close workers who didn't see eye to eye: The sons of Korah reach an unpleasant end when they oppose Moses; Saul could have made it easier for David if he had agreed a smooth handover; Judas chooses quite literally to do the devil's work despite being on Jesus' team; Paul and Barnabas argue over the involvement of John Mark so badly that they part company; John has to reprimand Demetrius for his attacks on the church.

It is easy to think you are on the same page, when in fact you are in different paragraphs or even different chapters. Bill Hybels, senior pastor of Willow Creek Community Church in the northwest suburbs of Chicago, uses the illustration of the friends who rejoice that they have decided to enter the restaurant business together. Trouble is, one wants to have an American-style diner, another Chinese and another Indian. Although sharing a very similar vision, there must be specific agreement if the restaurant partnership is ever to work.

So there will be times within any church where members will need to clarify what it is they are aiming for. Such conversations are not easy, but unless we bite the bullet, little can be achieved. The vision may need to be adjusted; some may need to leave in order for goals to be accomplished.

5. Pray for the leaders
If you don't believe the leadership of the church are supportive of your desire to follow Christ as He is leading you, be sure to pray for them. They serve the Lord as your leaders so are worthy of respect and honour. They may have misunderstood what you are about. They may fear that your efforts at kingdom work may overshadow theirs. If your dream involves others, they may suspect that you secretly want to drag

people away from the church to your scheme. This happens. So you may need to reassure them of your motives. Hopefully you can stay, and be an influence for good.

6. Get support from elsewhere

In his book, *Winning with People*, John C. Maxwell wryly notes: 'when it comes to people, there is good news and there is bad news. The good news is that some people in your life are going to be the source of your greatest joy. The bad news is that those same people may be the cause of your greatest problems.'[3]

If you suspect that there are no like-minded fellow travellers in the church you attend, then there are some ways of keeping your vision strong, even while still attending. You can link with co-stars, you just won't ever meet them! The co-stars you link with will be via various media, from books and magazines to radio, TV and the Internet.

Some of my strongest influences have been through books, tapes, CDs and iPod downloads. My thinking has been lifted, corrected and reshaped. My heart has been warmed and my vision enlivened. Many have 'kept themselves going' in unresponsive church settings, and though it is not ideal, if the choices of alternative input are limited, it is a necessary lifeline.

7. Find someone you can help

If you want to really understand something, one of the best ways is to pass it on. You don't need to be setting yourself up as 'the great teacher' but there's nothing to stop you spending time one on one, or with a small group reading a Gospel and discussing what you find. Indeed, these people don't have to be Christians!

Many years ago I met an American missionary who was at the time based in Austria. His name was Floyd Schneider and he told me that he spent his time skiing and sailing with non-Christians, which sounded like a fun way to live out your calling. He went on to explain that his intention was to get to know people so that they would ask him what he, an American, was doing in Austria.

It was then that he would invite them to read John's Gospel with him. As they read they would have questions, which he would refuse to answer! He would tell them to read on, knowing that God would be speaking. God had used him to plant one church using this method and he was just starting his second! He is now serving in Washington State back in the US. His book outlining the approach is called *Evangelism for the Faint Hearted*.[4] Buy it and see what I mean.

Your next step

If you spend all your time with people who are lacklustre it is easy to sink to their level of passion and commitment. It is those who share your desire to grow that will be the most support. If you haven't linked with co-stars already, I recommend that this is a priority. I would urge you to consider carefully where you attend. Take your time and ask God constantly what you should do. Remember, even if the whole church isn't your cup of tea, there may be a small group on your wavelength – that's all you need. It could just be the difference between you flourishing in playing your part in God's story, and finishing this book leaving it on the shelf and wasting your life. Which probably sounds blunt, but I owe it to you!

Summary

1. God's design is that we link with co-stars as we live our part in His story.
2. Ideally you need to find people who share your vision for the kingdom, have a strategy to see change, can relate at a deep level and give honest feedback on your progress.
3. Many churches will not have the characteristics you seek. There are approaches which can help you grow even if you don't feel the environment is ideal: remember we are all flawed; share your vision wisely; seek to understand; confront issues; pray for the leaders; get support from elsewhere; find someone you can help.

Action

1. If you are not part of a local church, why not consider joining one? Log on to www.eauk.org/churchsearch/ and type in your area.
2. If you feel no one in your church understands your desire to be serious about God, make some discreet enquiries with the church leaders. Offer to hold a prayer meeting at your home, or start a study group. You could even use this book as a starter.
3. If you are struggling with fellowship, do you have old friends you could contact? Ask them to pray for you.

Consider

1. When was the last time someone spoke into your life?
2. Is it likely to happen? Why? If not, how can you get closer to other Christians so that it is possible?

Notes

1 Stanley Hauerwas and William H. Willimon, *Resident Aliens: Life in the Christian Colony* (Abingdon Press, 1989).
2 Stephen Covey, *The Seven Habits of Highly Effective People* (Free Press; First edition 1990).
3 John C. Maxwell, *Winning with People* (Nelson, 2004).
4 Floyd Schneider, *Evangelism for the Faint Hearted* (Touch of Design, 1994).

06
FIND YOUR ROLE

FIND YOUR ROLE

Your part will include specific roles which only you can play. You can find them by discovery, experiment, talking to others and talking to God.

Actor Michael Caine was asked how he decided on which roles to play: 'First of all, I choose the great roles, and if none of these come, I choose the mediocre ones, and if they don't come, I choose the ones that pay the rent.'

The life of the actor or actress may sound incredibly glamorous but the reality is that it is a job like everything else. Every leading role, or award-winning performance, has probably been preceded by months awaiting an agent's call, auditioning and that nervous wait to hear if the face fits the part.

As you look at finding your role or roles within God's story you can be forgiven for sharing something of an actor's apprehension. What specifically does God have in mind for you? Maybe you are familiar with tales of people happily enjoying a comfortable life in suburbia only to discover that God wanted them to go somewhere they didn't want to go to play a role they didn't want to play. Or maybe it is just the fear that you will be forced to do something you really hate: speak in public, give your testimony to sneering teenagers or live in a country known for poisonous spiders.

So how can we find the role God has for us?

Live as an apprentice of Jesus

You may be a little surprised that 'Find your role' is Chapter 6 of a book subtitled *Discovering your part in God's story*. Why isn't this earlier on? Everything we have looked at so far has been about learning from Jesus how to be like Jesus in your daily life – whatever that means for you; every hour, every minute. This is what being under God's reign is about. Wherever you are, wherever you go and whatever you do, you have the opportunity to spread light and goodness as the fruit of your interactive relationship with Jesus.

As you look at the Gospels and the New Testament – as we have done in earlier chapters – you will see that disciples learn how to live for Jesus and see apparently normal situations as occasions for God's will to be known and seen. They are defined by being apprentices of Jesus – this would be the 'occupation' in the passport. So, if you list your roles and station in life now, you will identify the roles and stations that God intends for you in order to be involved in His story, as His apprentice. These are the areas in which He intends for you to be like Jesus – work, play, romance (which could also be either work or play or both!), parenting, studying. Simple, eh?!

I start with this perspective on finding your part because many get confused into thinking that 'their role' is primarily about something that God drops into their lap, or which happens in the four walls of the church – an idea assisted by ministers who see what happens there as all-important. Church is an important arena, certainly, but it is actually just a gathering of people who know the reign of God in their lives. Your part, as theirs, flows from your interactive relationship with Jesus wherever you are so that you regard any arena as a place where God's will can be seen and known. It is just a case of seeing yourself as a Christ follower in whatever you are doing and asking what there is about your activity that can be changed because you are under God's reign and rule.

Your character is of crucial importance because it goes with you wherever you go! Bill Hybels, senior pastor of Willow Creek Community Church, Chicago, says that he learned to appoint people on the basis of the 3Cs: first character, then competence and finally chemistry with him and the rest of the team: 'I didn't always place character above competence but I do now. I have learned that at an occasional lapse in competence can be accepted but lapse in character creates problems with far-reaching implications.'[1]

Let's remember that many of your roles will be the same as many other people's – as a son or daughter, as a brother or sister, as a husband or wife, as a parent or guardian, as an employee or employer, as a citizen. In some of these cases you have a massive influence within that role which you need to take seriously. For example, never say, 'I am just a parent!' As nineteenth-century lawyer and poet, William Ross Wallace, said about mothers: 'the hand that rocks the cradle rules the world.'[2]

Whatever our role, Jesus says in John 13:34: 'A new command I give you: Love one another. As I have loved you, so you must love one another.' We are to love and serve others, seeking to encourage those around us to be all that God wants for them.

- How do you see your roles?
- Can you see yourself as a Christian in those roles?
- What would have to change for God's rule to be known in the roles?

Finding the special role

Leaving aside the way in which we are to serve as disciples in whatever we are doing and in whatever role we have been given – what about the particular things God has for us? How do we find those?

As you read this, it may be that you already know. I have a good friend who knew the moment he came to faith that God was intending him to serve as a preacher. A lifetime as a preacher in church and itinerant settings throughout the UK has confirmed this. But most find the discovery of their role takes a bit longer and involves prayerful thought. Here are six places to be sure to look. One or more may be particularly relevant for you.

1. Look back

Your past is a great clue to finding what God is looking for you to do. 'Your story' is shaping your life more than you realise. In his book, *To Be Told*, Dan Allender encourages readers to examine their lives in a search for the story that God is telling through their existence. Allender says we often don't know our own stories because we doubt their existence, dismiss their importance, or we're distracted.

> *Too many people are missing their story because they're watching the stories of others. We live vicariously through television, sports, magazines, and talk shows. Such stories may occasionally educate us, but most often they sedate us. They free us from admitting that*

*our own life is dull and lifeless. They attract us because they offer
life without risk. They are deathly safe.*[3]

Too true. A preoccupation with soaps, novels, or sport on TV may be
a good sign that you are missing out on drama elsewhere. Far too much
of my life has been spent getting my dramatic kicks through watching
men kicking a bag of wind or hitting a little white ball with sticks.

Your story is not confined to the bin just because you have woken
up to God's. The part He has for you will, in part, be shaped by your life
up to this point. In some cases your past will have a significant impact.
How many cancer sufferers who are healed go on to found charities to
raise money for cancer research? How many former addicts are back
helping those who are in the same predicament they were in? Part of my
motivation for writing this book is that I have had to think deeply about
my part in God's story. It may be that God has already enabled you to do
things in His kingdom that are an indicator of how He might use you.

However, in some cases, the past has an opposite effect. We steer
well clear of situations we disliked, that tempted us, or that we are still
talking to our therapist about! But even negative experiences can be
helpful. Knowing what we are not equipped for is a good thing. Would
that people in the wrong roles learned these lessons earlier!

2. Look within

a) Strengths

A research project by the Gallup organisation found that only 20 per
cent of people feel they get a chance to do what they do best every
day at work. The research is the basis of a bestselling book by Gallup
ex-chair Donald Clifton and British-born Marcus Buckingham, *Now,
Discover your Strengths*.[4] It says that the idea of sticking to what you're
good at should be the foundation for management. You are better
off discovering the strengths of your employees and using them,
than spending money and time on training them to improve their
weaknesses. In other words, forget about being well-rounded. If you
don't speak Spanish, don't try to learn. If you don't seem skilled at
selling your products to seniors, don't try to force it. Instead, become
a lopsided but phenomenally successful specialist.

It all makes eminent good sense of course. You wouldn't ask BBC's *Weakest Link* presenter Anne Robinson to be a counsellor; Virgin's Richard Branson to do a desk job; or impressionist Rory Bremner to announce the trains at a railway station. (Though the latter might be fun.)

It is worth looking within because it is easy to miss the obvious. What has God placed within you already? If you have a natural talent, it may be that God is intending this to be expressed, either in your daily work or in your spare time. A little thought and prayer might lead you to discover ways in which this is part of God's story for you. Christians have been traditionally sceptical of natural strengths – fearing that we will end up relying on ourselves and not God. It is a legitimate concern but, providing we acknowledge in humility the source of the strengths and our dependence on God, there's no reason why we can't rejoice in what He has already placed within us.

And if you are not too sure what your strengths are, you might want to check out *Now, Discover Your Strengths* (mentioned opposite) which details different ways to measure strengths. Many Christian churches and charities have used these measures to great effect. As well as explaining the rationale, the book also gives you a questionnaire which charts your signature strengths: the thirty-one character types listed include achiever, competitor, communicator, learner, empathiser and maximiser.

You are unique. No one else has your combination of talents. Providing you submit them to God they can define your impact on the world.

b) Temperament

Looking within can also help us reflect on the temperament we have been given. God has wired us up in a certain way so that we view our world differently from others. There are many ways of measuring temperament but perhaps the most widely used personality indicator in the world is the Myers Briggs Temperament Indicator (MBTI). The inventor, Isobel Myers, concluded that there are four primary ways people differ from one another. She labelled these differences 'preferences' – drawing a similarity to 'hand preferences' to illustrate that although we all use both of our hands, most of us have a preference for one over the other, and that one takes the lead in many of the activities in which we use our hands.

Briefly, the four temperament differences outlined in the MBTI are as follows:

1. **Extroversion (E) or Introversion (I)**. Everyone has two faces. One is directed towards the outer (extrovert) world of activities, excitements, people and things. The other is directed inwards to the inner (introvert) world of thoughts, interests, ideas and imagination. One of these faces is more dominant.

2. **Sensing (S) or Intuitive (N)**. The sensing side of our brain notices the sights, sounds, smells and all the sensory details of the present. It categorises, organises, records and stores the specifics from the here and now. It is reality based. The intuitive side of our brain seeks to understand, interpret and form overall patterns of all the information that is collected, and records these patterns and relationships. It speculates on possibilities, including looking into and forecasting the future. It is imaginative and conceptual. Each of us instinctively tends to favour one over the other.

3. **Thinking (T) or Feeling (F)**. The thinking side of our brain analyses information in a detached, objective fashion. It operates from factual principles, deducing and forming conclusions systematically. It is our logical nature. The feeling side of our brain forms conclusions in an attached and somewhat global manner, based on likes/dislikes, impact on others and human and aesthetic values. It is our subjective nature.

4. **Judging (J) or Perceiving (P)**. All people use both judging (thinking and feeling) and perceiving (sensing and intuition) processes to store information, organise thoughts, make decisions, take actions and manage lives. Yet one of these processes (judging or perceiving) tends to take the lead in our relationship with the outside world while the other governs our inner world. A judging style approaches the outside world with a plan and is oriented

towards organising one's surroundings, being prepared, making decisions and reaching closure and completion. A perceiving style takes the outside world as it comes and is adopting and adapting, flexible, open ended and receptive to new opportunities and changing game plans.

To fully grasp your Myers Briggs preferences you can use simple questionnaires on the Internet but it is better to see a trained Myers Briggs consultant who gives you the 'preference indicator' (it is not a test) and will talk through the results, explaining the degree to which each of the four options is true for you – you might be ENFJ but borderline I–E for example.

Indicators such as Myers Briggs or Strengthsfinder are just tools to help you. They are not intended to label or define you and they are not essential. What really matters is that we are becoming Christlike, not that we have filled in questionnaires in a certain way and been given a set of results. If you are functioning in a loving community you should find that you are understood and accepted without needing to know how you like to live. But these resources are a reminder that God has made us a certain way and that He will likely use what He has put into us for His kingdom. A small investment in a book or course might just help you to 'look within' more effectively.[5]

3. Look to others

In Chapter 5 we focused on the importance of joining with co-stars to fulfil our role. The Church is simply a gathering of people who are under Christ's rule and we ideally need to connect with a local one. We have noted already that we mustn't restrict our role to this arena, but as it is God's instrument on the earth to effect change and see His kingdom spread, the church will be a key place in which we play our part.

As well as particular strengths and temperaments, we note there are three passages in the Bible which list what have become known as 'spiritual gifts' (1 Cor. 12; Rom. 12; Eph. 4).[6] These 'gifts' represent the ways in which God, by His Spirit, works in the believer's service in such a way that they are able to accomplish things for the kingdom which they could not do with their own power. The lists in 1 Corinthians and

Romans 12 suggest that everyone has received at least one gift and that we need to value the way God has made and equipped every believer.

Spiritual gifts are like natural abilities, and there may be some overlap with the strengths mentioned earlier in this chapter. But they are more than natural abilities and in some cases (as with, say, prophecy, tongues and healing) there is clear evidence that God is involved. See the list at the end of the chapter.

Spiritual gifts are not to be confused with spiritual fruit (Gal. 5) which describe our character development. You can have a gift but have no character, just as you can be ace at the violin but lousy to have in the orchestra!

We need to 'look to others' because they can help us discern and understand the ways in which God is equipping us to serve Him. We are often the last people to spot how God has equipped us, because it is 'natural' to us. The gifts are given to build up the believers God has placed us alongside, so they are the ones who can tell us whether our contribution is any help or not! I don't believe the lists in the Bible are meant to be exhaustive. The exhortation within the 'spiritual gifts' passages mentioned above is that the body of Christ will be the poorer if we don't spend time experimenting and serving with our spiritual giftings.

When seeking God on what gifting you have, I would especially note unsolicited comments that you didn't expect, from people who weren't obliged to say something kind or affirming. You might want to reflect on how you want to serve people, given the chance: those with the gift of mercy want to teach it to others, teachers want to give instruction, leaders want to take people somewhere. Often we discover that we have a range of gifts, though there is typically a major one that stands out. In some cases, not only is the person gifted, but they have a ministry to the church using the gift which requires them to leave paid employment in order to practise it more widely.

Although it is possible that God may reveal to you or other Christians your gifting, it is more likely through activity that you will discover what God is doing. How would you discover whether you had the gift of healing if you didn't ever pray for the sick? How would you discover a mercy gift if you stayed away from people in trouble? Having a gift doesn't mean we won't benefit from training and practice. A person who is a gifted preacher can benefit from basic help on delivery, use of notes, preparation, voice and appearance for example. A leader can benefit from feedback on their leadership style and approach.

4. Look out

Many Christians are happy to look in and around and back, but it is often in looking out that our part is brought into focus. Remember the end game. We are participating in a movement of change that will last beyond this present age. We need to look out on our world and ask, given the gifts and passions that God has given us, where should we be at work?

It has been often said, 'the need is not the call'. But that doesn't mean it has nothing to do with it. A friend who was passionate about helping children, visited a village in India and was so shocked by what he saw that he set up a charity, The Child's Trust, to meet the need. Another guy I met was concerned about the many in the UK who have short-term needs of food and clothing while waiting for the social security system in the UK to provide benefits. So he set up The Food Bank. These were people who 'looked out' and saw a mesh between gift, temperament and passion and sensed a nudge from God to do something that extended His reign in an area where His name and work were not known.

There are some exercises at the end of this chapter to help you look out and see whether there are areas which might be calling you to use your abilities.

5. Look up

All our self-analysis is done as we look up – talking to God about the part He wants us to play (though, naturally, He is in us and around us and not just 'up'!). God may have a direction He wants us to take that is a complete surprise. God can sometimes use the most unlikely and unexpected people to do things that are outside their gift zone, areas of expertise and background.

Look at Moses and Paul. Moses is educated in Egypt – where many historians say writing was first developed – and so God uses his abilities to write a good chunk of the first five books of the Bible. Paul is a Pharisee, schooled in the Law, so God brings him to faith and uses him to lead churches and pen a good chunk of the New Testament. Both of God's choices 'make sense'.

But take Nehemiah and Peter. Nehemiah is in Persia as a cup-bearer to the king. Odd preparation for leading the people in a wall-building project? It seems that the pertinent factor here is that he has the ear and the trust of the emperor and is therefore given leave and the means to make a difference. Peter, one of the apostles, is an unschooled fisherman. Yet he is sent to be the apostle to the Jews; while Paul, the Jewish scholar, is sent as apostle to the Gentiles. And although unschooled, Peter winds up writing two books in the New Testament and assisting Mark in writing his Gospel.

So, for all our self-analysis, we may find that God's role for us makes little apparent logical sense, but it is God's way of furthering His purposes. This isn't permission to be wild and wacky in what we try, but it is recognition that it is God's kingdom we are operating in and that any activity done in His power and strength may just surprise us.

6. Look ahead

At the age of twenty-one I had been preaching for three years. I was part of a church that believed in giving opportunities to anyone they regarded as gifted. But I had reached the stage where I realised that I was unlikely to make much progress in preaching the Bible if I didn't spend some concerted time studying it. I had already become limited in the range of the things I said and I was clueless about how I could preach from the Old Testament, which made my range even smaller. I decided that fitting in study in the evenings would be tricky and so I opted to attend London Bible College (now London School of Theology) for a year, though in the end I opted for two. I am glad I did.

It may be that you too find that you cannot fulfil your role in God's story without giving some serious thought to developing your skills and knowledge. It may not be a year or more at Bible college, it may be evening classes or weekend courses, correspondence courses or directed reading by a wise Christian leader. Some baulk at the idea but, when you think about it, much of life includes periods of sustained specialist learning – so why not Christianity?

Do you learn to drive without lessons and some time spent reading *The Highway Code*? If you want to improve at sport you need regular, focused activity. Jesus spent three years with the disciples. It's no surprise that we may need to set aside some time for God to prepare us for His work.

Action!

God made you for drama, for making a difference and impact on your world, so that when people attend your funeral they will rejoice in a life well lived in God's service which has had an impact that stretches into eternity. Sound like something you might want to enter?

This chapter has involved lots of questions. It is worth reviewing them prayerfully if you haven't done so as you have been reading. You can waste hours of time and lots of energy if you pursue areas which do not reflect 'your part'.

Remember the story Jesus tells about the talents and the importance of using them? Check it out in Matthew 25:14–29. The most depressing part is the guy who, despite being giving a part to play, ends up being thrown into outer darkness because he failed to realise the goodness of the landowner and the importance of using what he had been given. This is not a model to emulate.

Here are some questions to consider. You will need to take your time. If you are tempted to read on at this point, I suggest you make a note that you will need to return to these questions when you are in the mood to do so.

1. Look back
- Have there been times of great joy or pain which have made you who you are today?
- Is it possible that God may want to use what you have learned to help others?
- What gets to you?
- What work or leisure activities have given you the greatest satisfaction?

- What situations have come your way which you have had to handle?
- If you could change one thing about life what would it be?

2. Look in
- What sort of things would you like to think God has for you in His service?
- Are there things that so captivate you that you easily lose track of time?
- What stirs you?
- What makes you angry?
- What galvanises you to action?
- What do family members or colleagues compliment you on? (Assuming it is that sort of environment!)

3. Look to others
- Do you know your spiritual gifts? As you look at the list at the end of this chapter, do you think any fit you?
  (You may need to spend time with other Christians who know you, or use a spiritual gifts assessment course such as Network.[6])
- When you are with other Christians how do you instinctively want to serve?
- Who do you admire?

4. Look out
- If you know your gifts/strengths, is there a particular group that you are drawn to serve? The elderly? The sick? The displaced?
- You may be a leader. What do you want to lead? A small group? A church? A soup kitchen? A kids' football team?
- In the book of Acts, the gifts of apostleship, prophecy, miracles, healing, evangelism, teaching, mercy, service, knowledge and wisdom are all used for the benefit of people outside the kingdom. Who can you bless with your gift, who doesn't know Jesus yet?

5. Look up

- Have you spent time asking God what part He wants you to play?
- Are you ready for anything?
- What fears do you have?
- What reassures you?

6. Look ahead

- If you are sure of the answers to some of the questions above and know the sort of role God has for you, is there training that you need to find out about?

My conclusion

1. At this stage I am not sure what specific role I am to play:

   I need to do more work   I need help   I need to pray

2. At this stage I think the following role(s) may be on God's heart for me:

   ....
   ....

3. At this stage I am fairly certain I should be doing this:

   ....
   ....

4. I know what I should be doing but I don't know where.

5. I know what I should be doing, and where, but I'm not sure how I will get there!

Summary

1. Your primary role in life is to be a growing follower of Christ. All other roles in family, work and leisure flow from this base.

2. In discovering the role(s) God has for you, there are six places to look:

- Look back – how might your past be a clue?
- Look in – what strengths and temperamental preferences have you been given?
- Look up – are there things that God is impressing on you?
- Look around – how do you naturally react to the body of Christ? What do you do that edifies others?
- Look out – what particular needs in the world around you do you see that God might direct you to address?
- Look ahead – what training might you require?

Action

Work through the questions above if you haven't done so already.

Consider

1. Why do so many Christians have no idea what their role should be?
2. How many people in your church do you think know what their strengths and gifts are?

Notes
1. Bill Hybels, *Courageous Leadership* (Zondervan, 2004).
2. William Ross Wallace, *What Rules the World?* (1865).
3. Dan B. Allender, PhD, *To Be Told* (CWR, 2007).
4. Marcus Buckingham and Donald Clifton, *Now, Discover Your Strengths* (Free Press, 2001).
5. Contact CWR to find out when their next look at the Myers Briggs Temperament Indicator is scheduled for. Phone: (01252) 784700.
6. Spiritual gifts, The book, *Networking*, which looks at spiritual gift discovery is available from Willow Creek Association UK & Ireland, PO Box 966, Southampton SO15 2WT. Phone: (0845) 1300909. Website: www.willowcreek.org.uk.
   And CWR's resource 'Discovering Your Basic Gift' is available as a free download from www.cwr.org.uk/downloads.

The spiritual gifts listed in the New Testament are:

Romans 12
exhortation
giving
leadership
mercy
prophecy
service
teaching

1 Corinthians 12
administration
apostle
discernment
faith
healing
helps
knowledge
miracles
prophecy
teaching
tongues
interpretation
wisdom

Ephesians 4
apostle
evangelist
pastor
prophet
teacher

In addition
celibacy (1 Cor. 7:7)
hospitality (1 Pet. 4:9)
martyrdom (1 Cor. 13:1–3)
missionary (Eph 3:6–8)
voluntary poverty (1 Cor 13:1–3)

07

PUT YOURSELF INTO THE ROLE

PUT YOURSELF INTO THE ROLE

Modern society believes that denying self is the hardest thing you can ever do, but it is the vital key to not only finding your part but playing it with all the strength God provides.

I had finished a round of golf and, not for the first time, wondered why I bothered to play the game at all. Like many golfers I have had a love–hate relationship with the game since I took it up twenty-five years ago. There's the sheer beauty of a crisply struck iron, with the ball curving through the air settling inches from the hole, and the rank ugliness of the shot that barely goes further than the divot! I was fed up: I was either going to get better, or sell the clubs.

So I visited a golf professional whom I knew offered advice based on taking a video of my golf swing and talking me through what I was doing wrong. This had worked before; it might work again! I spent five minutes hitting balls from a mat in the pro's bay at the driving range. The pro wasn't as negative as I expected. He showed me a video of my swing and explained why what I was doing meant the ball didn't fly as far as I wanted it to. He froze the video of my swing and compared it onscreen to a section of a video of the three-time major golf championship winner, Ernie Els, captured at the same moment in his swing.

'There's your problem right there,' he said, like a doctor pointing at an X-ray. He showed me the position of Els's club head compared to mine as the club head reached knee height on its way to hit the ball. I could see that Els's was perfectly poised to deliver the maximum power to the ball. The angle of my club was maybe 45 degrees different.

'That's where you are losing it all, just there,' he repeated, pointing to my frame.

He then proceeded to suggest a number of swing exercises to help me become a little more aware of where my club head was, so that I could approximate to Ernie Els's position. This involved, rather bizarrely, practising swinging the club holding the club head with the wrong end!

His analysis proved to be enormously helpful, and although Ernie has little to worry about in the way of competition, I went back to striking the ball firmer and straighter than I ever had. I would continue playing, until the next problem …

As you consider your part in God's story, there is also a small detail you need to grasp if you are to fully enter into what God has for you. It is the failure to grasp this detail that could lead new Christians to finding that 'Christianity doesn't work!' I refer to the subject of self-denial, something that has been implied already in earlier chapters and is worth focusing on specifically. Self-denial is not exactly a top subject in most churches – about as appealing as a survey of prohibited foods in Deuteronomy, or talks on the minutiae of the tabernacle in the book of Exodus. You may be tempted to skip this chapter, but not only is it a vital aspect of playing your part in God's story it is actually excellent news, in spite of its bad press.[1] The Christian life is literally, 'a life to die for'.

We have already touched on the theme of self in our discussion of certain subjects:

- We are made in the image of God and as such have some of God's essential qualities within us. The 'self' God made was good.
- Our self is turned in on itself. We don't enjoy the dependent relationship with God that He intended. Self is corrupted.
- When we come to faith in Jesus we are 'born from above' – God's Spirit makes our spirit alive. We are freed to be the people God intended us to be. Self is being renewed.
- We learn to be in God's kingdom; we are apprentices of Jesus learning from Him how to be like Him. Self is made up of mind, heart, soul and body and is being re-shaped.
- We have turned away from writing our story in order to be part of God's bigger story with Him as co-author. Self has a new context.
- We need activities that will help us break free from old ways. We need to be freed to take on new behaviours prompted out of a heart that is moved towards God's story. Self is hidden in Christ.

This sounds like a pretty radical makeover – the before and after shots are going to be very different! So why is self-denial 'good news'?

What self-denial isn't

Avoiding fun

The bad press for self-denial comes because most Christians presume that it is about you denying yourself pleasure for fear that it will lead you into sin. It is a well-motivated concern, though it almost seems that, in a perverse way, Christians come to enjoy it. They stay away from the cinema, sporting events and leisure entertainment that might be regarded as worldly, and have such a tight rein on money they only shop for second-hand clothes and furniture. The behaviour spreads – within some church circles an unconscious peer pressure dictates what is and isn't acceptable: a clapped out Mini is OK, a BMW certainly not. Margate is OK for a holiday, but not Malibu.

The apostle Paul was quick to dismiss teaching that gave people unnecessary burdens. Advising his young friend, Timothy, who was serving the church in Ephesus, Paul refers to people he believed were led astray from following Jesus:

> *They forbid people to marry and order them to abstain from certain foods, which God created to be received with thanksgiving by those who believe and who know the truth. For everything God created is good, and nothing is to be rejected if it is received with thanksgiving, because it is consecrated by the word of God and prayer.*
>
> 1 Tim. 4:3–6

If you want to shop for second-hand clothes in a Mini, that's fine. But don't pretend it is because God wants you to. Throughout the New Testament, Paul is quick to spot those who believe there is virtue in 'self-denial' their way. Becoming stricter than God doesn't make you more holy – it simply screws you up!

Putting ourselves down

Others presume that self-denial is about refusing to accept any appropriate praise and thanks for anything they have done. One preacher afflicted with this attitude, refused to be thanked for a sermon, responding, 'Oh, it wasn't me, it was the Holy Spirit.' To which the church member replied, 'Oh no. It wasn't that good!'

There is an appropriate humility that is the mark of someone who recognises their gratitude to God. The apostle Paul says:

> *For who makes you different from anyone else? What do you have that you did not receive? And if you did receive it, why do you boast as though you did not?*
>
> 1 Cor. 4:7

Boasting is out, but a calm and joyful appreciation of how things have gone is good and healthy. Putting ourselves down does not lift God up, but fails to value what He has done in us.

What self-denial is

The key to joy

Self-denial has to be understood in the context of joining in with God's story as people who abandon their story to follow His. It is part of the liberation we find as new people, indwelt by the Spirit, now freed to serve the living God. Jesus tells His disciples:

> *'If anyone would come after me, he must deny himself and take up his cross daily and follow me. For whoever wants to save his life will lose it, but whoever loses his life for me will save it.'*
>
> Luke 9:23

An army officer could legitimately say to a recruit: 'Unless you give up your life as a civilian you cannot be a Royal Marine.' No one would think the officer was being harsh and elitist; the one follows the other. Jesus is not saying to us, 'I am putting the bar of behaviour deliberately high – unless you deny yourself, you are not coming onto my team.' He is saying, 'unless you deny yourself you won't be able to be on my team.' Jesus is just stating facts about the nature of spiritual life.

Unless I gave up being single I couldn't be married. I denied myself singleness to be with my wife, and haven't regretted it for a moment! Jesus carried a cross knowing that He was going to die. It is a horrible image but illustrates the total abandonment to the new life that comes from following Jesus. He offers 'a life to die for', as we die to self we live a new life in Him.

Rob Bell, in his book, *Velvet Elvis*,[2] explains how the disciples would have viewed Jesus' call on their lives. Every Jewish boy learnt the Torah (the first five books of the Bible) off by heart, from the age of six. But by the age of ten only the very best graduated to the next stage. This cut-off point was like the age of sixteen in British education, except that there was minimal chance of going on to tertiary education. An elite group went on in their studies at around the age of fourteen, and then an elite group of that group would ask to join a rabbi. The rabbi would decide who would join him and selected only the very best. Once under a rabbi's oversight, a Jewish boy would literally become like the rabbi. It was not just knowledge education, but life education: how to speak; how to interact with others; how to do the practical things in life. This vision of change was so compelling that the student denied himself in order to imitate the master.

When Jesus calls His followers to leave their occupations to follow Him, He is instituting an alternative education system for them. You didn't need to be a member of the elite – anyone, even fishermen who dropped out early from their education, could be trained. The disciples were not thinking, 'Oh no, of all people He has selected me!' But rather, 'Wow, He believes in me and is taking me on!'

So these men discover just what that training means. They find a rabbi who is unlike other rabbis. (We repeatedly read in the Gospels that people say Jesus taught with 'authority', unlike other teachers.) His teaching hits home and is backed by physical demonstrations of the kingdom of God: the powers of the age to come are being seen in this world. Here is someone who is so close to God that He knows what God wants and does it. Something of heaven is seen on earth. God is showing His glory in the lives of ordinary, irreligious, messed-up people.

Today, the spatial dimension is removed – we don't follow a physical Jesus but we still follow His teaching. And the added bonus, not available to the first followers, is that God Himself is quite literally 'in on the act' through the Holy Spirit within our lives.

Our role today is to follow Jesus by daily learning from Him how we can live as if we were Him: in the supermarket, at the gym, in school, mucking out pigs. It involves our whole selves, our thinking, our feeling, our choosing, that reaches down to our very souls, as we saw in Chapter 4.

It's vital for progress

Understanding and practising self-denial is the crucial part of the Christian life that many miss. They assume it is only for the elite, hardy and specially called. Wrong. We are all specially called. You are giving up your life (your story) but will always win. You give up a life that is heading for an eternity without God, for one where He reigns – a life to 'die' for.

Paul, writing to believers in Turkey, said:

> ... just as you received Christ Jesus as Lord, continue to live in him, rooted and built up in him, strengthened in the faith as you were taught, and overflowing with thankfulness.
>
> Col. 2:6–7

Being rooted and built up will mean many things. God will use what we read in the Bible and hear explained to us. He will use Christians around us who model a walk with Christ and cause us to think. He will use our reactions to circumstances. He will whisper to us through our conscience and in our minds as we start to understand more of what He says.

So when people ask the question, 'What will I need to give up to be a Christian?', it is the wrong question. No one can give an answer to that question. You need to learn from Jesus how to live your life as He would live it if He were you. In conversation with Jesus, something legitimate for one person is a stumbling block for another. He will tell you what you need to give up.

As I was growing up I had an interest in football. I lived for football at school. My ability at football was a large part of my identity with my mates and my impact on the world. I read about football, played football, watched football on TV and travelled by ferry from the Isle of Wight to Southampton on the south coast of England, to watch my Dad's team in Southampton, even though I supported Everton. If Everton lost, my weekend would be ruined (which was all too often in the 1970s!). Now, there's nothing wrong with all that, and it was great that my brother and I could spend quality time with Dad. But football had become a god. God has no downer on football, but for me it had reached an unhealthy level. If my commitment to Christ at seven years of age was to mean anything, I needed to get a grip on it. I talked to God about it, realised the folly of following football as a god and gave the game back to Him. In the event He used the game – some significant friendships have been formed through it and, no longer sold on it, I am able to enjoy it much more (when the team wins that is …).

But idols can come in unexpected forms. I host a programme on leadership for Premier Radio,[3] where I interview Christian leaders. I recall interviewing Carson Pue, who runs Arrow Leadership in the US, about some of the dangers of leadership. He identified leaders who become addicted to spiritual experiences, ie they became addicted to how they felt when they were serving God in public. The feeling had replaced God in their affections. If meeting with God can become an idol, anything can!

It allows God to work

We noted earlier that a failure to understand and practise self-denial is at the heart of many Christians' problems. If you want to try and write your story your way, you can. You can write God out of the equation, and God – the ultimate spiritual being who has your good at heart, and would hold nothing from you that is for your good – will leave you to it. He won't go where He is not wanted.

In his book, *Christ in You*,[4] Charles Price tells the story of his wife Hilary's puzzling escapade with a lawn mower. Keen to do her bit she started the cylinder mower and proceeded to cut the grass in the back garden. Half an hour later she slumped exhausted on the garden chair and surveyed her work. She realised she had cut a mere fraction of the grass which Charles would have done in the same time. Charles relates how she knocked into the mower in frustration and accidentally engaged the switch connecting the mower to the power, which promptly shot off across the lawn dragging her with it! She had mowed the lawn, but not with the power provided by the mower!

As I reflect on my Christian life, I realise that too much time has been spent mowing my lawn without engaging the power. I have put in the effort and learned to do what works in respectable Christian company, but I have often missed looking to God, who promises His assistance.

God doesn't promise easy progress but the struggle sees forward momentum as our best efforts are allied to God's work alongside us. The apostle Paul put it like this: 'Work out your salvation with fear and trembling, for it is God who works in you to will and to act according to his good purpose' (Phil. 2:12–13). We push the mower – we must do our part – but God provides the power.

The great thing about God is that He is extraordinarily gracious and uses even our mixed motives and weaknesses. Sometimes it is three steps forward, two steps back! But we will make the most progress towards likeness to Jesus when we learn from Him and leave things behind that He tells us to leave. And we will know and see more of God's reign, in situations and people that concern us, when we look to Him. Dallas Willard has a saying: 'God wants to get you to the point where He can empower you to do anything you want.'[5] He is quick to underline that He does mean 'you', not 'He', because we are to be co-workers with God. We write the story together. Our will is changing so that we will what He wills. It will take time, and most of us can't yet be trusted with the power God longs to provide us with to do His work. However, you can say that you are in Christ, seated in the heavenly realms with Christ, co-heirs with Christ, indwelt by the Spirit of God. And you will discover that His plans and purposes for you are way beyond anything offered by a self-help guru.

Put yourself into it!

How do you make sure you don't fall into the trap of many Christians who undervalue or diminish the self-denial element?

1. Focus correctly

When we looked at getting fitted for our role we noted that we cannot effect change directly. This is particularly true when it comes to the self-denial that Jesus talks of. Self-denial is the result of a focus on the good news of God and the changes that Jesus promises as we put our confidence in Him and learn how to live our lives in the light of His direction.

How you choose to think is your first freedom, as we saw in Chapter 4. The apostle Paul tells us to put to death whatever is of the earthly nature (Col. 3:5). 'Count yourselves dead to sin but alive to God in Christ Jesus' (Rom. 6:11). Our mindset is to act as if we are dead to the things that Jesus says are unwise. In Romans 12:1, Paul says we are to be transformed by the renewing of our minds, which I understand to mean that we need to be convinced of God's Word in our heads, so that it permeates our lives. This will feel like a battle. We often keep the old life on a life-support machine as if we are fearful that the new one won't work. To follow Paul's teaching, we must starve the old life of oxygen and feed the new one with the best nutrients: the Word of God, prayer, worship, and so on.

Let's imagine that you sense that Jesus is seeking to work on your forgiveness. Someone has done something to hurt you; when you mentioned it to them, they were dismissive and refused to apologise. You feel angry with them, can't forgive them and imagine scenarios in your head where they come out badly. So how do you focus correctly? You know that forgiving is for your good – Jesus wouldn't have asked you to do it otherwise – but in all honesty you feel you should be annoyed and don't want to let them off the hook that easily. The key comes as you realise that you are to forgive others as God has forgiven you (Matt. 6:14). Their actions towards you may not have been nice or legitimate, but this is the fruit of their fallenness. You too make mistakes and need others' forgiveness. One day the tables may be turned. If God has forgiven you all your sins (and He has) then you can extend forgiveness towards them. You deny 'yourself' the right to feel annoyed but, as is often the case with self-denial, you will also experience freedom. As someone put it, 'bitterness is drinking the poison yourself and expecting your enemy to be ill!'

As you start to think correctly about the situation you should find that you start to feel differently about it. It is only after you think differently that your will is also liberated to act differently – whatever that may mean, from phoning them up to say something (if appropriate) to putting them back on your Christmas card list!

So, as your mind is filled with the goodness of God and you see the beauty of His good and perfect will, you will bit by bit see the world as God sees it and automatically deny self and live for Him. You may be taking small steps at the moment, but hang on in there – each step is a sentence in the story you are writing with God. You are getting a taste for a new drama and a new adventure. Soon the old story will be like last year's fashion, stale bread or adolescent humour that fails to raise a smile. Your nature will change and God's story will become more and more delightful. You will find that denying yourself enables something far better to grow in your life, and it won't feel bad.

Is there an area where you suspect you need to deny yourself? How can a correct focus help you do what you know you need to do?

2. Be relaxed about being wrong

When we read the Gospels we find that the disciples get it wrong time and time again. Jesus gently teaches them, helps them learn from their experiences and points out how things might be different next time. Self-denial means that we have Learner plates on and don't get too precious about our deeply cherished views on politics, lifestyle, relationships and leisure. Everything is up for grabs. It follows that regular Bible reading and reflection and occasional periods of longer Bible study are a vital part of our growth. So read the Bible with a pencil and highlight parts where you are told to do things you don't like, or have an opinion that is different from your present one. Get used to changing your mind. It's OK. In time you will start to be so saturated by God's view, it will become second nature.

What are your cherished opinions? Are you willing for these to change?

3. Abandon outcomes

Perhaps the biggest struggle we face comes when it is not so much a change in character we are battling with, but a change in situation. You want X but you can't have X. X is not sinful, just not for you at the present and you are confused because X seems eminently suitable. As you read this you may have already substituted X for something you know: freedom from illness, a baby, success in a job interview, a girl or guy you are keen on saying 'yes' to an offer of a relationship, or marriage. It may even have apparent kingdom benefits: you want to serve in a particular role, you want a charity to succeed, you want a ministry set up in your church. But the answer seems to be 'wait', or the answer seems to be 'no'. If you are facing a painful time as you read this, you will know what I mean. The sense of wanting seems overwhelming and you find it hard to believe that God doesn't want the same thing.

But you can trust God, who will bring all things together for good, so that you abandon outcomes and that feeling that 'I must get my way'. This is the secret of peace. You and I only see the short term and a small part of the picture. God knows what granting your request would lead to. It may be that He has a better plan that you will one day realise; it may be that He is teaching you character and trust. It may be that there are things He is doing in you through this that are for your good. And, it has to be said, you may never see the purpose of this. This may be one of those events which your non-believing friends claim prove that 'there is no God'; though, of course, you know better!

If you don't trust God, then anger and bitterness will fill your heart when the outcome doesn't turn out as you expected. Your life is in Christ; it is safe and secure and all that God does in and through you is for your good. You feel what you feel and you take it to God; He understands and knows your pain. If you feel hard done by, remember that many people face unanswered questions without any assurance that God is at all interested. At least you can look at the many things He has done for you and seek a peace inside which helps you through the pain, knowing that He does indeed do all things well.

4. Keep practising the disciplines

Self-denial is aided when we deliberately abstain from things we enjoy. This may seem that I am contradicting my criticism of those who seem bent on being deliberately miserable. What I am suggesting is that small periods of abstinence will break the grip of the small and larger addictions that make self-denial so tough. The fact that some people have gone over the top on self-denial does not mean they weren't on to a wise thing.

The disciplines looked at in Chapter 4 are to do largely with the body. We noted that we have been writing our story ourselves for so long that our body is primed to our will. This is how we operated from the day we learnt to scream for food. And some people have seemingly made little progress! Disciplines help to break the grip; they are activities within our power that enable us to do what we couldn't otherwise do.

Take fasting. If Jesus spent forty days in prayer and fasting in solitude, it wouldn't be a bad thing for us to spend time doing this ourselves! We find that God does something within us as we fast for Him, focusing on His will and His ways. Abstaining from food occasionally – a meal or for twenty-four hours – is something we do in our power that can help us more easily break free of other strangleholds. Fasting from food may be an obvious suggestion, but what about fasting from TV, shopping, sport or the Internet?

As we practise the disciplines, over time we will find that our grip on self is loosened and we are now primed for God's will. The sloth or gluttony (I must have X or I will die!) that characterised our lives is disappearing, and when God says jump, we do so and enjoy it.

The redeemed ego

An example of what is possible is provided by Billy Graham, the American evangelist who has preached to literally millions of people, and along with the Pope is one of the best-known religious figures throughout the world. Thousands have come to faith through him. In their book, *The Leadership Secrets of Billy Graham*,[6] Harold Myra and Marshall Shelley relate a story told by Graeme Keith, Treasurer of the Billy Graham Evangelistic Association and a lifelong friend.

*I was on an elevator with Billy when another man in the elevator
recognised him. He said: 'You're Billy Graham aren't you?'
'Yes,' Billy said.
'Well,' he said, 'you are truly a great man!'
Billy immediately responded, 'No. I am not a great man. I just have
a great message.'*

In the introduction to his autobiography, *Just As I Am,*[7] Billy Graham
says:

*If anything has been accomplished through my life, it is God's doing,
not mine, and he – not I – must get the credit.*

This is your aim: to get increasingly to the point where you will
what God wills and He empowers you to serve in His kingdom, like
Billy. It was Jim Elliot, the martyred missionary to the Auca Indians,
who said: 'he is no fool who gives what he cannot keep to gain what he
cannot lose.'[8] Those who presume that self-denial is the fool's choice
have understood little of human nature and nothing of the purposes
of God. As you read this book, imagine the living God looking at you
and seeing you in Christ. Your sin is dealt with. Your life is hidden with
Christ in God. You will battle and struggle but, when you do, that's the
'old' you still struggling. The new you is being renewed daily. Believe
it, accept it, rejoice in it and you will find that the denial of self, which
seemed so tough at first, really is part of the good news that Jesus said
it was.

Summary

1. Self-denial is a key element in our growth as a believer and,
   though it doesn't sound like it, it is good news!
2. It is not denying ourselves what we enjoy or putting ourselves
   down.
3. It is part of our discipleship, vital for development and allowing
   God to work.

4. To make sure self-denial is part of your life, you are wise to: focus correctly; be relaxed about being wrong; abandon outcomes; and keep practising the disciplines.
5. God wants you to become the sort of person whom He could empower to do what you (and He) want.

Action

1. Reflect on times when you have needed to deny yourself for a greater good.
2. Does this help to motivate you to learn to make self-denial part of your life?
3. Practise saying, 'I was wrong about that', in the next week. Do you find it easy to admit to getting things wrong?

Consider

1. Is it really a sacrifice to give up something in order to gain what Jesus offers?
2. Look at the parables in Matthew 13:44–46. What do they tell you about the joy of self-denial?
3. If God wants to empower us to do whatever we want, why is the development of a humble character so important?

Notes

1. There are people for whom the discussion on self-denial might seem especially odd. Developmental psychologists tell us that our ego needs to develop for us to be healthy individuals. The whole process of 'self-denial' presumes that I know who I am, know right from wrong, and have an ability to want good things for myself, namely a relationship with God in Christ. But there are those who have not had a normal development. They have become trapped so that they are not free to choose. Talk of their ego getting in the way of following Christ seems superfluous because they believe their low self-esteem prevents them from pushing themselves forward into any self-assertive situation. If this is you, my advice is that you speak with a counsellor or mature Christian to discover the source of the problem and find steps to recovery.
2. Rob Bell, *Velvet Elvis* (Zondervan, 2005).
3. *The Leadership File* on Sundays at 2pm on Premier Radio – archived versions at www.premier.org.uk
4. Charles Price, *Christ in You* (Kingsway, 2001).
5. I heard him say this on a visit to London in 2002, but also in other talks heard on CD. You can hear audio recordings of his excellent teaching at www.dwillard.org, plus details of articles and books.
6. Harold Myra and Marshall Shelley, *The Leadership Secrets of Billy Graham* (Zondervan, 2005).
7. Billy Graham, *Just As I Am* (HarperSanFrancisco; New edition 1999).
8. Elisabeth Elliot, *Shadow of the Almighty* (HarperSanFranciso, reissue 1989).

08
RECEIVE DIRECTION

RECEIVE DIRECTION

God doesn't hand you a set script for your life but expects you to grow into the part and respond to His direction as your journey unfolds.

In the film, *Raiders of the Lost Ark*, one of the most memorable scenes is set on the streets of Cairo. Indiana Jones' girl, Marion, has been kidnapped and Indiana Jones (played by Harrison Ford) is confronted by an Arab wielding a scimitar. The guy demonstrates his skills with the weapon, making sweeping movements in the air as if about to challenge Indiana to combat. It looks as if Indiana is about to join him in a duel. But instead the hero scowls, promptly brings out a revolver and shoots him, prompting laughter from the cinema audience. I was told by a friend that the original script indicated a whip fight between Indiana and the Arab. But, on the day of the shoot, Harrison Ford was feeling ill (both flu and diarrhoea were suggested) and asked if the scene could be shortened. The director, Steven Spielberg, said the only way he could shorten it was if Indiana pulled out his gun and just shot the guy. The entire crew laughed and that's how it was filmed.

Many films have moments when the director realises that something needs to happen differently. Illness, weather or malfunctioning props can all upset carefully laid plans and sometimes a scene on paper just doesn't work on set. The ability to 'direct' at such times is one of the reasons why directors such as Steven Spielberg are highly prized.

When it comes to your part in God's story it is important for you to know what to expect from God's direction. You are learning from Jesus how to become like Jesus. Does this mean that you get directions for every assignment rather as *Mission Impossible*'s Jim Phelps was given a taped message from the boss detailing the mission plans at the beginning of every episode? If not, what can you expect?

God's direction

God's clear interventions within the Old Testament vary from book to book. In some He speaks directly to individuals, and intervenes in their lives according to His unfolding purposes: to build a people who would know and love Him and show the world what He is like. In others there is no mention of direct involvement, though God is seemingly directing events behind the scenes (see, for example, Esther and parts of Nehemiah).

Some people received particular direction, notably the patriarchs in Genesis; Moses in the books of Exodus to Deuteronomy; Joshua; and the kings and prophets as Israel progressed as a nation. But the chief direction that shapes the Old Testament is in the laws given to Moses at Sinai. Indeed it was the success and failure in keeping the laws that would explain the history of Israel throughout the Old Testament. The Bible measured the success of a king's reign by whether he upheld God's laws or not.

At the end of the Old Testament, many of the books of the prophets begin with the phrase, 'The word of the LORD came to ...'. It often tells us where this took place, and in what year, and to whom it came, but interestingly doesn't always tell us how it came. Some received visions, some simply knew what to say, it would seem. It is almost as though there is an unspoken understanding that the way in which we personally hear God need not be described. The mode by which He speaks to us isn't what God wants us to react to; it is what He says that matters.

Now this may seem like ancient history and of little relevance to receiving direction today. But my point is that many of the characters in the Old Testament Scriptures received direction via God's written Word rather than a regular 'one to one'.

In the New Testament the Gospels give us the teaching of Jesus. He says: 'My teaching is not my own. It comes from him who sent me' (John 7:16). When Jesus leaves earth He promises that He will continue to communicate via the Holy Spirit and He teaches His followers about the kingdom through the Holy Spirit (Acts 1:2–3), even though He is present in His resurrection body. Throughout Acts we have God, by His Spirit, engaging with the apostles through visions, prophecies, the Spirit within, and circumstances. We read, for example, that the persecution forced many followers out of Jerusalem, to do what Jesus had actually commanded in Acts 1:8. In Acts 13:1–3 we read of the Spirit's direction in leading the Church to commission Paul and

Barnabas to leave Antioch and take the gospel elsewhere. In Acts 16:7 we see that the Spirit prevented the apostles from entering Bithynia. When Paul is in Corinth, God tells him in a vision that He is building His Church there (Acts 18:9–10).

God is a speaking God. It would seem odd, therefore, to conclude as some have done that He only makes silent movies today. His written record says He was regularly in touch with His people. His written revelation is His full and final word to the world, which anyone of any persuasion can read. But the living God still speaks.

So what of God's direction today? Is it God's intention that He should direct us every moment of every day and give us answers to our questions? What about the big decisions in my life? Do I text God and get a response straightaway?

God's intention

We saw earlier that God intends that you become like Jesus Christ. You are learning from Him how to live your life as if He were you. You will recall that God has chosen to be hidden from us for most of the time. He is not 'in your face', demanding attention. In the same way He is looking for you to learn from Him so that you can live your life. As your character changes (see Chapter 4) you will already be starting to make decisions that you know please God. It is not unlike the process of driving a car. You are probably at the stage where your actions have become automatic when you drive your car. Are you consciously thinking, 'Now I must depress the clutch to change into third gear'? Probably not. There have probably been occasions when you have driven home and can remember little or nothing about the journey! It has become what we call 'second nature'. In the same way, God intends you to grow so that many of the decisions you make will become second nature. He is looking for you to mature and grow. Parents might expect to warn their children about getting too close to the fire. But would those parents expect their children to still need warning when they are twenty-two?

In an average day you will make umpteen decisions, some more important than others. There won't be time to pray about every one.

But as you grow in your walk – seeing your thinking, feelings and choices develop properly within a body poised to do good – you will live as Jesus intends. It isn't 'specific direction' but it is no less precious. A father is prouder of a son who does the right thing knowing that he has chosen to do so because his character has been trained to that point, than if the son were merely doing it because he 'was told to'. God is pleased when we are mature enough to do as we know Jesus wants because we want to.

Read His directions

It follows that the primary need is for us to know what Jesus and the rest of Scripture has to say. Most of our daily direction is on public record in Scripture. Do I murder my boss? After all, he deserves it! Do I have a fling with my secretary? After all, she's lovely. Do I steal some serviettes from the canteen for my evening do? After all, they won't miss them. We don't need 'direction' in these cases: 'You shall not murder, you shall not commit adultery and you shall not steal' covers it! (Exod. 20:13–15).

But remember this is not the slavish following of rules, rather a participation in the life of God as we are enabled to do what God calls us to do. We are learning to be people who wouldn't want to murder the boss (even in jest), have a fling or pinch serviettes.

We have noted that before Jesus returned to the Father He gave a specific mandate in Matthew 28:18–20, which included 'teaching them to obey everything I have commanded you'. At the end of John's Gospel we read a similar exhortation:

> Jesus did many other miraculous signs in the presence of his disciples, which are not recorded in this book. But these are written that you may believe that Jesus is the Christ, the Son of God, and that by believing you may have life in his name.
>
> John 20:30

On both occasions, Matthew and John presume that the written record of the life and works of Jesus will be the primary mechanism for us to understand and live His life.

This is the pattern of teaching in the rest of the New Testament. Note the way those who followed Christ in the early years behaved:

> *Now the Bereans were of more noble character than the Thessalonians, for they received the message with great eagerness and examined the Scriptures every day to see if what Paul said was true. Many of the Jews believed, as did also a number of prominent Greek women and many Greek men.*
>
> Acts 17:11–12

The apostles urged their followers to be people of the Word. They wrote letters exhorting them to follow Christ; they didn't presume all would be well because they had received the Holy Spirit and therefore could manage without instruction. Paul advises Timothy in his first letter to him about how he should lead the church he was helping: 'Until I come, devote yourself to the public reading of Scripture, to preaching and to teaching' (1 Tim. 4:13). In his second letter he says: 'All Scripture is God-breathed and is useful for teaching, rebuking, correcting and training in righteousness, so that the man of God may be thoroughly equipped for every good work' (2 Tim. 3:16–17). At that time this referred to the Old Testament. Later in this book he urged Timothy:

> *In the presence of God and of Christ Jesus, who will judge the living and the dead, and in view of his appearing and his kingdom, I give you this charge: Preach the Word; be prepared in season and out of season; correct, rebuke and encourage – with great patience and careful instruction.*
>
> 2 Tim. 4:1–2

God's written revelation permeates the atmosphere of the New Testament, even at the time when the New Testament itself is being written (in the second half of the first century). In Acts, God speaks to the apostles, but we don't sense that every action has been directed by God, like a satellite navigation system in a car. They are not told which towns are likely to be hostile when they visit, or what exactly to expect in each day. Paul makes plans, but doesn't presume that God is in them (see Rom. 15:23,32). Often the apostles do what seems wise, or respond sensibly. They are not receiving a message-a-day, like an undercover agent in touch with base via a computer, but expect as mature believers to get on with the work they know Jesus has directed them to, namely inviting people to know the reign and power of God. As preacher Haddon Robinson puts it: 'When we ask, "How can I know the will of God?", we may be asking the wrong question.' The Scriptures do not command us to find God's will for most of life's choices nor do we find any passage instructing us on how it can be determined. Equally significant, the Christian community has never agreed on how God provides us with such special revelation. Yet we persist in searching for God's will because decisions require thought and sap energy. Instead of wondering, 'How do I find the will of God?', a better question to pursue is, 'How do I make good decisions?'[1]

Learn His voice

Some advice on guidance would stop there: you have the Word of God as all you need for life and godliness. But the history of the Church and the Scriptures themselves indicate that there are occasions when God does speak directly to us. This is separate from God speaking in the Bible; or God using a particular verse to 'speak' to us as we read it because it has some particular significance for our life circumstance. I mean us hearing God speak to us, one to one.

God spoke to the Church in Acts 13:1 indicating that Paul and Barnabas should be set apart for mission work. The Spirit prevented them from entering Bithynia. How does this happen? What do they mean when they say the Spirit told them?

The Bible gives no detailed explanation of how someone hears from God, but the witness of the Church down through the ages suggests that believers can know that they are hearing from God.

Jesus does tells us that the Holy Spirit will lead us into all truth, a reference doubtless to His work in helping the apostles teach the Church and, in two cases, write Gospels, but also a reference to His ministry in all followers.

This voice is rarely an audible voice, but more typically words which are in our mind that we know we did not generate and that we come to recognise as being put there by God. In *Hearing God*,[2] Dallas Willard says:

> All followers of Christ must be encouraged to believe that they can come to understand and distinguish the voice of God if they will but look within their minds for much the same kinds of distinctions within their thoughts and perceptions as they would find in the communications received from other human beings through spoken or written language: a distinctive quality, spirit and content.

Just as you get to recognise a human's voice through its quality, spirit and content, you can get to know God's voice too.

Let's look at these three in turn:

Distinctive quality of the voice

This concerns the impact it makes on our consciousness. It is a steady, calm sense of what God is saying. We learn to know that this is indeed God and not something we have dreamed up. John Wesley in a sermon entitled, 'The witness of the Spirit', says: 'How to distinguish light from darkness ... do you not immediately and directly perceive that difference, provided your senses are rightly disposed?' He implies that we can know the voice by its quality, just as surely as we know light from darkness.

Spirit of the voice

The voice is a voice of peacefulness, joy, confidence and sweet reasonableness. When God speaks in your heart it doesn't matter where your mind has been going; He blocks and overrides all circuits. What He says is right. His word has perfect balance and proportion. Everything He shows us fits together seamlessly. The word He gives us is complete. His presence fills us with well-being.

Content of the voice

The voice will always accord with God's nature and kingdom as made clear in the Bible. If you sense God telling you to do something expressly forbidden in Scripture you know it's not Him. Paul says:

> *For this reason, since the day we heard about you, we have not stopped praying for you and asking God to fill you with the knowledge of his will through all spiritual wisdom and understanding. And we pray this in order that you may live a life worthy of the Lord and may please him in every way: bearing fruit in every good work, growing in the knowledge of God ...*
>
> Col. 1:9–10

Just as we come to learn the voice of a friend, so the learning of God's voice is an art to cultivate. You may not spot it immediately; you may come to realise that God had spoken but you didn't realise it at the time.

Become attuned

It goes without saying that a regular programme of getting to know the Bible is vital. You can read the Bible in a year, looking at three or four chapters a day in twenty-minute sections. For example, the NIV Bible-in-a-year format will get you through the whole Bible. Even if you don't recall very much, you will still get to know and sense what matters to God and what doesn't, and it will help you spot the daft from the divine when it comes to your thinking. It is the primary way the people of God learn to walk like Jesus did.

But in the course of this life in the kingdom, you will also be talking to God about all of life: the sales call you are about to make, the visit to the elderly relative, whether to accept a freelance project, which options to take for GCSE, whether you should subscribe to *Gardening Weekly*. For the most part, you will be part praying, part thinking – you are setting things before God, reflecting on anything in Scripture that might have a bearing, using your reasoning, your feelings and your hopes. You practise what the Scriptures call 'praying without ceasing'.

Willow Creek Community Church's Senior Pastor, Bill Hybels, speaks of asking God to reveal insight even when He is communicating with someone.

> *'Sometimes I will be talking to someone and they'll be telling me everything is OK and the Spirit will whisper to me: "They are not OK".*
> *'And I'll go, "Hey, how are you doing really?" Then all of a sudden it will come out.'*

That may be part of his gift mix and not everyone's. But God can give you insight whenever and wherever.

For most of the time you will find that you get on with life without any particular words from God. If you are uncertain, you may set a situation before Him, maybe asking a question before going ahead and making a decision. Sometimes there will be a deadline and so you tell God what you intend to do, providing He doesn't indicate otherwise. You know that if any of these decisions matter particularly to God He will know how to let you know.

But as you pray, or subsequently, you may indeed think, 'I am not going to do that after all'. You have changed your mind. Was it in response to prayer? Maybe. You may never know. You do know that you consciously committed it to God and went ahead and did what you thought best as His child.

Or, you may have a sense in your thinking that 'this is what I need to say' or 'this is what I need to do' and there is something about what you are now thinking which is different from your previous thoughts. You sense this is God's answer. Now, at this point you don't run down the road shouting, 'God spoke to me! God spoke to me!' Or even necessarily tell your closest Christian friend. You may be wrong. You tell the Lord you think this is Him and what you intend to do or say as a result.

On other occasions you may not be about to do anything in particular. You have no decision to make, or concern that you are wrestling with. But you sense something in your thinking that you come to recognise as God. It may be a phone call to be made, it may be to hold back from doing what you had decided a few weeks back to do.

So you talk to God about it and tell Him what you intend to do.

You are God's child. He loves you. You are learning from Jesus how to live and to be a co-worker with Him in the story He is writing. You believe Him to be almighty, with all power and all authority, and so you trust Him to lead you daily in this way.

It makes sense therefore to give specific time each day for prayer and Bible reading, sometimes known as a 'quiet time'. You spend time alone and in silence to give Him room. Some people may find that God doesn't speak to them even after giving Him opportunity, or that there are long periods where they sense nothing. This needn't be alarming. If you work for a boss and know what you are supposed to do, you don't need him to give you directions every day. In the same way, God may be trusting you to get on with the life you are living, having trained you how to live.

Those who are worried that God has not said anything to them might be surprised to discover that it is precisely because God is happy with them that He is quiet! They are learning to, as John Stott famously put it, 'think God's thoughts after Him'. And God is happy that they are growing as His child.

Consider circumstances

Direction through circumstances is a tricky business. There was the man who visited the missionary committee convinced that he was being called overseas to serve God.

'That's great,' said the chairman, 'so where has He told you to go?'

The man looked crestfallen. 'Oh I am not sure,' he said woefully.

'Well, when He has told you, come back and see us,' said the chairman gently.

A month went past and the man was back with the committee. 'Did God tell you where He wanted you to go?' asked the chairman.

'I believe so,' said the man nervously.

'Where is it?'

'Well, I was praying as I was walking and I looked up and there was a billboard advertising Brazil nuts, and so it came to me, it's Brazil.'

To which the chairman replied, 'It's just as well it wasn't an advert for Mars Bars!'

The story sounds incredibly foolish, but isn't so far from the mark. I confess that in the early years of my Christian life I was afflicted with 'spiritualisingitis' – the ability to see the most extraordinary links in events that I presumed must be God's direction.

Looking back, it was immaturity. I wanted God to direct me and tell me what to do so that I would avoid pain or difficulty. But God wanted me to trust Him to be with me whatever the eventuality and trust Him even in my decision-making process.

Circumstances will indicate certain courses of action, but not in the way we might imagine. We have seen already that our past, gifts, temperament and strengths are already circumstances that will dictate our future course of action. As you weigh up a course of action, then it may be that a situation changes as you pray about it. You are looking for a house in a certain area and an ideal house comes on the market. You have a need for dental treatment and receive a surprise cheque from an aunt. You are wondering how to talk about Christianity with a friend and discover they are reading *The Da Vinci Code*. These are circumstances that inform your decision and that you may see as an 'answer to prayer'. But none of them in and of themselves are 'proof that it was God'. None force you to act. You may conclude that the house wasn't ideal, the treatment not necessary, and discover the friend couldn't get beyond the first fifty pages of *The Da Vinci Code*! Circumstances are merely one of the aspects that you can consider when making a decision. They certainly serve to frame what may be possible and will often reflect God's sovereign oversight of your life, but be wary of reading too much into them. Remember, in many cases God is calling you to make a wise choice. He doesn't have a secret plan that you have to prise out of Him, but wants you, as a growing follower, to do what you think is best, trusting that He will intervene in your thinking if He needs to.

So, circumstances rarely overrule your need as a child of God to act wisely and must never suggest a course of action contravened by God's Word.

Check with friends

God is looking to develop a conversational relationship with you, so you need to develop the art of listening and reflecting. You have a loving Father who cares for you. But, that said, Scripture encourages us to check things out with those who know us well and care about us. We are far from being infallible and can become confused into thinking that God has spoken when we have just been engaged in 'wishful thinking'. When I worked at *Christianity* magazine, John Buckeridge, the Senior Editor, received regular enquiries from people who said that God had told them to put all their savings into producing a Christian magazine. He tried to be as gracious as he could in outlining the considerable set-up costs and the ongoing costs of operating in a saturated market which has recently seen some major magazines folding. Often they went ahead anyway, sent him the first copy and, surprise surprise, discovered it was the only print run they could manage! So don't mortgage your house to fulfil your dream for the kingdom just yet. Chat with friends. Ask them to pray with you. And if your plans involve any need for financial or prayer support from church, talk sooner rather than later.

Sometimes someone will believe God has spoken to *them* about you. You are wise not to rule this out. But remember, you still need to decide what to do with this. We are told not to treat prophecies with contempt (1 Thess. 5:20) but also to weigh prophecy (1 Cor. 14:29). Is it really likely that God would go to them and not speak to you?

In Acts 16 we read:

> *When they came to the border of Mysia, they tried to enter Bithynia, but the Spirit of Jesus would not allow them to. So they passed by Mysia and went down to Troas. During the night Paul had a vision of a man of Macedonia standing and begging him, 'Come over to Macedonia and help us.' After Paul had seen the vision, we got ready at once to leave for Macedonia, concluding that God had called us to preach the gospel to them.*
>
> Acts 16:7–10

The word 'concluding' seems almost unnecessary. They had just had a vision! But their reasoning powers were not redundant. The vision was not a done deal but required the group as a whole to 'conclude' that this was what God was saying. You are wise if you check with others before making big moves, even if you have received a vision!

Summary

1. As someone learning from Jesus about the kingdom, you can expect to receive direction.
2. His primary means of directing you will be via His work from within, through the Bible, so as your character changes you instinctively will do what Jesus would do.
3. He will also speak to you directly when and if He needs to. You can learn to sense when He is doing this.
4. You are wise to spend time regularly talking to God and committing situations to Him so that He has opportunity to speak with you.
5. Circumstances will sometimes guide you, but beware of reading too much into them. You still need to decide.
6. The counsel of wise friends will help you stay on track and discern whether your thinking is really God-directed or not.

Action

1. Get into the habit of talking to God about your life, even about things you may have thought were trivial.
2. Ask God to help you listen out for His voice. Ask Him specific questions and then wait and see whether, in whatever way He chooses, you receive a reply.

Consider

1. Is it possible that you would receive more direction if you sought it more?
2. Can you think of a time when God led you specifically?

3.   What about your last twenty-four hours – how has God's Word informed your behaviour?

Notes

1 Haddon Robinson is quoted by Gary Friesen, *Decision Making and the Will of God* (Multnomah, 2000).
2 Dallas Willard, *Hearing God* (IVP, 1999).

09
LEARN TO IMPROVISE

LEARN TO IMPROVISE

Life rarely goes the way you expect it. Don't be deflected from playing your part by the tough times which will come your way.

Experts have ranked it the number one speech of the twentieth century. It was delivered by rights activist, Martin Luther King Jr, on 28 August 1963 from the steps of the Lincoln Memorial in the US capital during the March on Washington for Jobs and Freedom. There were some 200,000 marchers present, 20 per cent who were white, and it is regarded as a defining moment in the American Civil Rights Movement. Known worldwide as 'I have a dream', the speech expressed perfectly the aspirations of King and the many Americans, black and white, who wanted an end to racial division. But what few know is that the wording of the speech was changed by King as he was speaking. Deep into his sixteen-minute address, King began to improvise, drawing on his experience as a preacher. 'I have a dream that one day this nation will rise up and live out the true meaning of its creed: "We hold these truths to be self-evident, that *all* men are created equal,"' he said. King, who was only thirty-four, had used the 'I have a dream' phrase in other speeches, but never so stirringly or so memorably. It was only when he saw the crowd and their sense of expectation that he realised he needed to change what he had prepared if he were to make the impact that he wanted.

This ability to improvise to meet the situation is a crucial part of the armoury of many leaders. The ability to 'think on your feet' can mark out the great from the good, not just in public oratory but in their dealings with life. It is a skill especially prized and admired in the acting profession. *Whose Line is it Anyway?* was an improvisational comedy show which was transferred from the radio onto British TV. The show consisted of four performers and comedians who created characters, scenes and songs based on audience suggestions or pre-written prompts from the host. The results were hilarious and showed the skill of actors and actresses in creating humour without preparation.

But you don't need to be a comedian or civil rights activist to improvise. We all do it all the time. In fact, if someone is unable to improvise away from their life script we know that they are suffering from some sort of disorder. Life does not turn out the way we expect. People behave strangely. Accidents happen. Life knocks you for six. As you look back on your story you will be able to identify this; you may even think your life thus far has been full of surprises. The epitaph, 'It wasn't what I expected', could be written at the end of many lives.

The surprise factor can throw people who seek to follow Jesus. Many have been sold Christianity on the lie that 'it will all be OK' now that you come to Christ. God is all powerful and can make it good for you now that you have sided with Him.

As we have seen, Christianity is good news, but not in the way some preachers tell it. There is no promise that the life you lead will not involve heartache and pain and struggle. Some have given up on this version of Christianity, claiming God did not help them in their 'hour of need'. They prayed for healing and their friend died. They asked for help with a decision and things got worse.

For those with no faith in God, the complexities of pain and suffering become just another reason for rejecting any higher being that is involved in this world. They shrug their shoulders and make the best of things, or they become bitter and angry at the human condition.

Those who have faith can have more problems. They have to answer the question, 'How do I integrate what has happened into my world-view and belief that God is good and loves me?' It is a version of the question of the book entitled, *Why Do Bad Things Happen to Good People?*

More specifically, my concern in this chapter is to look at how what happens to you is integrated into your part in God's story. Sometimes you are not sure that you like the story He is writing!

Thinking biblically

We saw in Chapter 4 that our desire to learn from Jesus how to live as if He were us includes learning to think as Jesus thought. It means learning to see life differently.

Bad events can cause a number of reactions:

- We catastrophise – Oh no, things are going downhill from now on.
- We personalise – God is trying to say something to me, this would never have happened if I hadn't …
- We minimise – So what? I am not going to pay any attention to this. Let's move on.
- We fantasise – Maybe something similar is going to happen.

It obviously depends on the precise event as to which reaction is strongest. Exactly the same bad event can cause wildly different reactions depending on what we believe the event signifies. A simple stomachache for one person is 'cancer', but for another it is 'time to take some Andrews Liver Salts'. Someone who loses their job may shrug their shoulders philosophically, while another feels that it's 'the end of the world'.

We have already seen in Chapter 8 that circumstances can be indicators that God is speaking to us, providing we don't use them as the only measure. So how do we think 'biblically'?

1. This is God's world
Jesus taught His followers to believe that this is God's world and an excellent place to live and grow in relationship with Him. He taught them that 'God's kingdom' is at hand. God is good and has good things in mind for them. They can enjoy living in the flow of a walk with God. Just as God cares for His physical world so He will care for His followers.

The enemy's tactics are not dissimilar to the ones he used with Eve in the Garden of Eden: 'You can't trust God, He doesn't have your best interests at heart.' He can get you believing that your latest catastrophe or problem is the sign of worse to come.

We each have the daily choice of which voice we believe. The events that happen to us and around us are to be simply included as part of God's story as it is written in and through the life we live. We see life through God's spectacles.

2. But the world is a mess
Jesus also taught His followers to be aware both of their own failings

and the evil in the world. In what is known as 'The Lord's Prayer' (Matt. 6:9), He says they should pray that God's rule might be seen around them, just as it is seen in heaven itself. He taught them to pray that they would not be put into situations where sin becomes more attractive than God's way. He also reminded them that they would need God's help: 'Deliver us from evil.'

Thinking biblically means learning to put our first thoughts Godward when the messiness of the world is evident. The phone call telling you bad news, the test results revealing the need for surgery, the rejection letter in the post, all become an opportunity to trust Him and know the life that is in Him, rather than the pseudo life we try and create for ourselves.

So, in the midst of a bad event we can say: 'Lord how are we going to handle this? How can I learn and grow and see good come out of this rather than evil?'

Thinking biblically flows from the character change we looked at in Chapter 4. My mental default mechanism typically points towards fearful godless reactions. It can take a while before we learn to think Christianly. Our bodies are primed to react to the messages we are telling ourselves. A sense of panic, fear or tension can be upon us before we know what's happening.

I am not pretending we can flick a switch and slip into singing a chorus when bad news comes. But as we spend time practising the things Jesus practised, we will find ourselves slowly weaned away from these reactions: times reading the Bible and reflecting in prayer, times in solitude and silence, times with others talking through how we react, can and will enable us to react differently.

Alongside the mess, don't forget there are wonderful things to focus on every day, if we would do so. It has been rightly said that the atheist is at a loss for who to thank for a glorious sunset! Thinking biblically means thanking God for the glorious weather, the rain that waters the garden, the meal you enjoy, the painting you happen to see when you are out shopping, the skill of the orchestra playing in a concert, the pass that led to the goal, the timely phone call from a friend, the unexpected contact with a former colleague. As we struggle with why some things happen, we might also wonder why we're so blessed!

Keep your growth central

How do you feel if a book you have written sells 15 million copies? This is what happened to Rick Warren, Senior Pastor of Saddleback Community Church near Los Angeles, California. Here's what he said following the year *The Purpose Driven Life*[1] was top of *The New York Times* bestseller's list:

> 'This past year has been the greatest year of my life but also the toughest, with my wife, Kay, getting cancer. I used to think that life was hills and valleys – you go through a dark time, then you got to the mountaintop, back and forth. I don't believe that anymore.
> 'Rather than life being hills and valleys, I believe that it's kind of like two rails on a railroad track, and at all times you have something good and something bad in your life. No matter how good things are in your life, there is always something bad that needs to be worked on. And no matter how bad things are in your life, there is always something good you can thank God for. You can focus on your purposes, or … you can focus on your problems. If you focus on your problems, you're going into self-centeredness, which is "my problem, my issues, my pain." But one of the easiest ways to get rid of pain is to get your focus off yourself and onto God and others.'[2]

Rick reminds us that it can be tempting to see the overcoming of problems as a detour in life's journey. We deal with them, frustrated that we are unable to get on with life. We even talk of 'getting life back on track'. I don't deny that a bout of illness, a business crisis, a house sale that falls through or a relationship break-up interrupts our sense of direction and purpose. But remember that as a follower of Jesus it all counts. If our aim is to learn from Jesus how to live, these apparent interruptions can become milestones that we look back on with gratitude. We keep our growth in Him central. In these times we are reminded that God is real – 'a very present help in trouble' – and rest on and in Him in ways that draw us closer to Him. As Warren Wiersbe says: 'the bumps are for climbing on!'[3]

In his excellent book, *The Divine Conspiracy*,[4] Dallas Willard writes of the golden triangle of spiritual growth. At the apex of the triangle is 'Action of the Holy Spirit'. At the two points along the base are: 'ordinary life (temptations)' and 'planned discipline to put on a new heart'. In the centre of the triangle are the words: 'Centred on the mind of Christ'.

When we looked at 'Plan for character change' in Chapter 4 we saw that it is impossible for us to grow without the Holy Spirit. We cannot change by willpower but can practise the spiritual disciplines so that God does what only He can do. The circumstances of life are the arena in and through which you grow and become centred on the mind of Christ: as you commute daily, as you face an awkward boss, as you relate to an awkward teenager, as you have time off ill, as you visit an elderly relative. This includes the so-called Christian meetings or times (church, Bible Study, prayer partnerships, quiet times, etc.) but must include the 95 per cent of the other times of life.

James says at the start of his letter:

> *Consider it pure joy, my brothers, whenever you face trials of many kinds, because you know that the testing of your faith develops perseverance. Perseverance must finish its work so that you may be mature and complete, not lacking anything.*
>
> James 1:2–4

The word for 'trials' is a broad one meaning the multicoloured details of life – everything from chronic pain to a friend's bad breath. Paul says a similar thing when writing to believers in Rome:

> *Therefore, since we have been justified through faith, we have peace with God through our Lord Jesus Christ, through whom we have gained access by faith into this grace in which we now stand. And we rejoice in the hope of the glory of God. Not only so, but we also rejoice in our sufferings, because we know that suffering produces perseverance; perseverance, character; and character, hope. And hope does not disappoint us, because God has poured out his love into our hearts by the Holy Spirit, whom he has given us.*
>
> Rom. 5:1–5

But God is able to build within us such fortitude (through the Spirit and our disciplines) that we have a deep abiding sense of 'it's OK' even as we suffer. We don't rejoice 'that' something happens, but we can rejoice 'in' it.

Peter too writes to Christians who were suffering persecution:

> *In this you greatly rejoice, though now for a little while you may have had to suffer grief in all kinds of trials. These have come so that your faith – of greater worth than gold, which perishes even though refined by fire – may be proved genuine and may result in praise, glory and honour when Jesus Christ is revealed. Though you have not seen him, you love him; and even though you do not see him now, you believe in him and are filled with an inexpressible and glorious joy, for you are receiving the goal of your faith, the salvation of your souls.*
>
> 1 Pet. 1:6–9

Each of these three passages (James, Romans and 1 Peter) suggests that suffering can be a reason for rejoicing if we see it correctly – as an opportunity for us to put more confidence in Jesus and thus enjoy the new kind of life that He promises. So as 'stuff' happens in our day, from the minor irritation to the major crisis, we can see it as serving the aim of seeing God's reign and rule coming more fully into our lives.

But I need to stress that this will only happen as we have mastered the spiritual disciplines and learnt to rely on the Holy Spirit.

Joni Eareckson Tada, speaker, author and head of the disability charity, 'Joni and Friends', gives a wonderful example of how she did this after a tragedy when she was seventeen.

> *One hot July afternoon in 1967, I dove into a shallow lake and my life changed forever. I suffered a spinal cord fracture that left me paralysed from the neck down, without use of my hands and legs. Lying in my hospital bed, I tried desperately to make sense of the horrible turn of events. I begged friends to assist me in suicide. Slit my wrists, dump pills down my throat, anything to end my misery! I had so many questions. I believed*

in God, but I was angry with Him. How could my circumstance be a demonstration of His love and power? Surely He could have stopped it from happening. How can permanent, lifelong paralysis be a part of His loving plan for me? Unless I found answers, I didn't see how this God could be worthy of my trust. Steve, a friend of mine, took on my questions. He pointed me to Christ. Now I believe that God's purpose in my accident was to turn a stubborn kid into a woman who would reflect patience, endurance and a lively, optimistic hope of the heavenly glories above.[5]

Whatever our circumstances, we can make them part of God's story. They are not a detour, but part of the pathway. You don't need to say, 'God sent them', to be able to say, 'God allowed them and will bring glory through them'. If Joni can come to rejoice through a diving accident, maybe you can see what God has for you in what you are facing?

Know when to take it personally

'Look, don't take it personally!' he said, having just had a go at something I had done. The words may be well meaning – he was assuring me that this incident did not define me in his eyes – but ultimately the words were futile. I was the one who had made the mistake. It was tempting to reply: 'So how else should I take it?'

On one occasion, the disciples asked Jesus whether it was appropriate for a man they met to take it 'personally'. In John 9 we read:

> *As he went along, he saw a man blind from birth. His disciples asked him, 'Rabbi, who sinned, this man or his parents, that he was born blind?'*
> *'Neither this man nor his parents sinned,' said Jesus, 'but this happened so that the work of God might be displayed in his life. As long as it is day, we must do the work of him who sent me. Night is coming, when no-one can work. While I am in the world, I am the light of the world.'*
> *Having said this, he spat on the ground, made some mud with the*

saliva, and put it on the man's eyes. 'Go,' he told him, 'wash in the Pool of Siloam' (this word means Sent). So the man went and washed, and came home seeing.

John 9:1–7

It was common in Israel at the time to believe that people's life circumstances were connected to sin. The rich were the blessed and those who were poor and in this case, blind, were being punished by God for their behaviour, or their parents' behaviour. The disciples presume that this man should take his sad circumstance 'personally'.

But Jesus says this situation has nothing to do with past misdemeanours. The good news is that He can do something about it. He has compassion on the man and proves that He is the Light of the World.

Later, this time in Luke 13, Jesus is asked about a tragedy that had made front page news.

Now there were some present at that time who told Jesus about the Galileans whose blood Pilate had mixed with their sacrifices. Jesus answered, 'Do you think that these Galileans were worse sinners than all the other Galileans because they suffered this way? I tell you, no! But unless you repent, you too will all perish. Or those eighteen who died when the tower in Siloam fell on them – do you think they were more guilty than all the others living in Jerusalem? I tell you, no! But unless you repent, you too will all perish.'

Luke 13:1–5

Jesus is saying we shouldn't assume these men were being personally judged; tragedies happen, our major concern is that we put our trust in God so that as and when they happen to us, we are ready. Those in the Western world need to take particular heed as we are inclined to think that because we don't face some of the life-threatening diseases people do in the two-thirds world, we are 'OK'. We're not.

Does that mean, therefore, that we never take anything personally? A belief that life's events can be connected to our behaviour does have biblical precedent. God does intervene in judgment when people disobey Him. God warns us of the consequences of certain behaviour and then acts accordingly. Israel knew that if they disobeyed there would be consequences – they ended up in exile for seventy years, an event that was chiselled into their collective memory. In the book of Job, the three 'comforters' were convinced that Job was being punished for something he had done.

There is also an indication in the New Testament that consequences of sinful behaviour should be taken personally. Jesus warns Peter that he will betray Him, knowing the pain that this will cause but reassuring him of His prayers and support (Luke 22:31–32). In the book of Acts, Ananias and Sapphira lie about the money they gave to the church and are struck dead (Acts 5:1–10). Paul wrote to a church in Corinth and warned them that misbehaviour at the Communion service had caused some to be ill and some to have died (1 Cor. 11:30–31).

Jesus Himself implies that some pain will come to you 'personally'. Indeed, alongside the promise of eternal life and His reward, Jesus promises His followers that very thing! Responding to the disciples' remarks that they had left everything to follow Him, Jesus replies:

> *'I tell you the truth … no-one who has left home or brothers or sisters or mother or father or children or fields for me and the gospel will fail to receive a hundred times as much in this present age (homes, brothers, sisters, mothers, children and fields – and with them, persecutions) and in the age to come, eternal life. But many who are first will be last, and the last first.'*
>
> Mark 10:29–31

If you are persecuted for your faith you can 'take it personally'! You are suffering for the sake of Christ.

The big question is: how do we know when 'to take it personally'?

1. Ask the Lord what you can learn from what has happened. Is it a consequence of what you have done or said? If it is, ask God's forgiveness and deal with any fall-out, such as apologising to people, making recompense, doing anything necessary to prevent a repeat.

2. If you don't think you need to learn anything, relax. When pain or struggle comes into our lives it is an opportunity to trust. If you are facing pain or struggle it will always be time to look to the Lord. Pain is a great way for us to focus, regardless of whether we know if it's 'personal' or not.

3. If people think they have the low-down on why it has happened, thank them for their concern but tell them firmly that God hasn't revealed this to you.

4. Remind yourself of God's love, care, goodness and ability to turn around bad situations (Rom. 8:28–29).

5. Ask close Christians to pray for you that you may bear what you are facing with good grace and learn to 'rejoice in all things'.

God does not play games with us and if we seek wisdom in a matter He will give it, and reveal what we need to know about it when we need to know it. And there will be times, as with Job, when we just have to trust Him. At the end of Job, after three chapters of speculation, God finally speaks in chapter 38 and says to Job (I paraphrase), 'Look, I am the wise one here. Trust Me!'

Live in the light of what you know

In his super book, *The Life You've Always Wanted*,[6] John Ortberg tells a story about Mabel, a resident of a nursing home, blind, nearly deaf, and suffering from a cancer that was hideously disfiguring her face. Bedridden for twenty-five years, with no known relatives, Mabel should have been bitter, uncommunicative and self-absorbed.

When he was a student chaplain, Tom Schmidt visited the hospital and presented Mabel with a flower. He imagined Mabel would be unresponsive. 'Here's a flower,' he said. 'Happy Mother's Day.'

Mabel pulled the flower close to her face, attempting to smell it and then, in somewhat slurred speech, said, 'Thank you. It's lovely. But can I give it to someone else? I can't see it, you know, I'm blind.'

So, Schmidt wheeled Mabel to another resident and heard her say of the flower, 'Here, this is from Jesus.'

'That,' said Tom Schmidt, 'was when it began to dawn on me that this was not an ordinary human being.'

As Schmidt's acquaintance with Mabel grew, so did his sense of awe. He felt each time he entered her room that he was walking on holy ground. Often he would read a scripture to Mabel and, from memory, she mouthed the words along with him. Then, she might break into a song praising God. 'I never heard her speak of loneliness or pain except in the stress she placed on certain lines in certain hymns,' Schmidt recalls. The student chaplain began going to Mabel's room with pen in hand, ready to jot down the amazing things that she would say.

During one week, Schmidt says, he was stressing out, thinking about exams at seminary and a million other things when the question dawned on him, 'What does Mabel have to think about – hour after hour, day after day, week after week, not even able to know if it's day or night? So, Schmidt decided to ask Mabel the next time he saw her. 'Mabel,' he asked, 'what do you think about when you lie here?'

'I think about Jesus,' she said. Schmidt said he thought for a moment about the difficulty of him thinking about Jesus for even five minutes, and then asked, 'What do you think about Jesus?' She replied slowly and deliberately ... 'I think about how good He's been to me. He's been awfully good to me, you know ... I'm one of those kind who's mostly satisfied ... Lots of folks wouldn't care much for what I think ... But I don't care. I'd rather have Jesus. He's all the world to me.'

If anyone had reason to just give up – on God, on Jesus Christ, on living – it was Mabel. But she didn't give up. She lived in the light of what she knew.

Tragedy and pain and suffering leave their mark. It may be that there will be times when we can't face prayer, or we feel angry with God. You may be able to make a list of confusing and painful things in your life that suggest there is no God or, that if there is, He isn't concerned with you.

Some of these times will be when you joined with God's story, when some of the turns that He took were utterly bewildering. You have a part to play in God's story. Don't allow pain or suffering to deflect you from what God is doing. Embrace it and, if necessary, learn from it and see it as part of life's richness. Putting your confidence in Jesus means remembering that certain things are still true – even alongside the puzzling stuff – and these things are more real and vivid, even if now a cloud is obscuring you from them. God created you. He loves you. The world's a mess because of evil but God is doing His renovation work, welcoming people from all around the world to join Him in His work of transformation. Jesus didn't only enter the world's sorrow, He tasted death so that you would not need to. He suffered more than anyone and He's working in and with you through and in spite of the troubles that come. He looks forward to that day when faith will give way to sight and you join Him in the new heaven and the new earth where righteousness dwells and there is no pain or tears, for the old has given way to the new, and the story that you are writing will continue into greater vistas and chapters even more glorious.

As C.S. Lewis says in his oft-quoted ending to *The Last Battle*[7]:

> *But for them it was only the beginning of the real story. All their life in this world and all their adventure in Narnia had only been the cover and the title page: now at last they were beginning Chapter One of the Great Story, which no one on earth has read: which goes on for ever: in which every chapter is better than the one before.*

Your part in God's story may involve the need to improvise, but one day you will know why, and then it probably won't matter. You will have a new story to live.

Summary

1. Life does not turn out as we expect. We all have to improvise.
2. Christians can allow the tough things that happen to them to deflect them from walking with Christ.
3. We can embrace the tough parts as our part of God's story if we have the correct attitude.
4. As we face life's difficulties we think biblically, keep growth central, know when to take it personally and live in the light of what we know. In this way we can look back on tough times as milestones when God did something special within us, and made our part in His story richer than we could have imagined.

Action

1. Look back on your life and note times of pain and suffering. Did they make you bitter or better?
2. Pray for someone you know who is going through a bad time. Ask God if there is anything you can do.

Consider

1. What makes it hard for you to improvise when things go wrong?
2. When you were growing up, did your parents or guardians improvise well? How has this affected your attitude today?

Notes

1. Rick Warren, *The Purpose Driven Life* (Zondervan, 2002).
2. Part of an interview between Rick Warren with Paul Bradshaw, quoted on various websites including www.southasianconnection.com
3. Dr Warren W. Wiersbe, *The Bumps Are What You Climb On: Encouragement for Difficult Days* (Baker Publishing, 1980).
4. Dallas Willard, *The Divine Conspiracy* (Fount, 1988).
5. Quote taken from the website www.powertochange.ie/changed/jeareckson.html
6. John Ortberg, *The Life You've Always Wanted* (Zondervan, 2004).
7. C.S. Lewis, *The Last Battle* (copyright © C.S. Lewis Pte Ltd, 1956. Extract reprinted by permission).

10
GET READY
FOR ACTION

GET READY FOR ACTION

Understanding how you can play your part today requires a vision of a new you. Would you believe it?

It was a classic sitcom in the 1990s that reflected the lives of six twentysomething friends – three men and three women – living in New York. It was called *Friends* and lasted for ten seasons, by which time the names of Ross, Rachel, Chandler, Monica, Joey and Phoebe had become as well known in the UK as Morecambe and Wise. The show's success meant the actors reputedly commanded $1 million a show. But few realise how much work went into the productions.

If a show was scheduled for a Tuesday, the preparation started on the previous Wednesday around noon.

Wednesday noon: Writers read through the script and decide what works. The network, the studio and the director give the writers whatever feedback they have. The writing staff spend the rest of the day and night doing a group rewrite.

Thursday: Actors work with the material, running through the whole show for the writers and producers. Actors receive feedback. Writers rewrite in the evening.

Friday: Run through for network and studio. Director and cast offer additional ideas. More rewriting at the weekend.

Monday: The director runs through the show with the cast, figuring out what his or her shots are going to be, finalising the actors' blocking, etc. Minor changes to script.

Tuesday night: They shoot the main situational set in front of a live studio audience.

Even then, post-production cutting, re-cutting and mixing the show could take anywhere from a week to three weeks, depending on how close to the air date they were.

That might sound a lot of work for a half-hour sitcom, but the sort of thing we might expect for a show as popular and successful as *Friends*. But even if you are not into acting, my guess is that you have done your fair share of dress rehearsals in your life. I am not thinking of acting particularly but the dress rehearsals you go through in your head.

It probably started in your youth: subconsciously you imagined acting out a favourite TV or film character when playing games with friends. As you grew older you imagined what you needed to do to get out of trouble, how to make and keep friends. In your teen years you anticipated asking a girl on a date, or responding to a request from a guy, or working out how to get him to ask you out. The truth is that most of us play through unconscious dress rehearsals. You need to imagine what you are going to do before you do it and if you cannot imagine wanting to do it, you are unlikely to do it at all. You tell yourself, that's just not me!

When it comes to living God's story, we need to imagine what it might look like to live the life Jesus would live if He were us. What is your part in God's story going to look like? Throughout this book there have been illustrations which I hope have shone light into this, but it is time to consider some people who have sought to live out their part in God's story so that you can get ready for action and, if necessary, script adjustments! They are a composite of various people's life situations that I have known. My comments after each are designed to provide 'coaching' based on the material in this book. You may find that you spot yourself somewhere!

Dave and the girl-free zone

When Dave became a Christian he was studying for a BA in Management and Business Administration at Reading University. He had had no previous knowledge of what he called 'serious Christianity' until he had arrived at university and discovered that people actually believed and lived the stuff that he had rejected at school. None of his mates at his comprehensive in Leeds gave Christianity any thought as a serious faith for the twenty-first century. But time spent one-on-one with a Christian friend on his course, reading through John's Gospel, had convinced him this was real and he found himself believing the Bible even before he made a formal commitment to follow Jesus after a talk at the CU. Living in hall at St Patrick's he was a keen member of the hall CU group as well as attending the main CU on the campus. But part of

Dave's old story was relating to the girls on campus. Like many young men, Dave had had various relationships and at twenty was no virgin. His natural mode was to spot a girl he fancied and try and get serious. He would flirt, see if there was any spark, and put on the charm if he thought the girl was at all interested. He knew he needed to get his sex life in order if he was to make progress. How would he do it?

Living God's story

We have noted that the old story can be firmly embedded within the depths of our personality. Dave could go for the legalistic approach – avoid women – which might work in the short term, but sooner or later he will have to face one! But what he really needs is change on the inside. He cannot choose to stop fancying women (which wouldn't be a good idea in any case!). He needs a heart that loves rather than lusts so that he feels appropriate desire without it consuming him. Jesus' teaching was that it was wrong to look at a woman in order to want to sleep with her, not that the idea should be expunged completely. Jesus wasn't advocating monasticism!

1. He will need to think correctly – looking first at what the Bible teaches about sex and love. He needs to want to change, not that willpower will work, but so that he wants not to lust but to love instead. Love wants the good of the other – how could he learn to want their good and not his way? This involves understanding that God is his strength. God made him to find pleasure in relationship, chiefly with God, and maybe one day with a woman, but in the meantime, it is not the end of the world if he has to learn self-control. God does promise to provide all he needs for life and godliness.

2. But Dave will have to act. Unchecked, the raging hormones are likely to win. This may mean spending time alone for a while, reflecting on his life and how he typically behaves. He might want to set aside a half-day. But this is not a time for lots of introspection. After his 'retreat' his time is to be spent depressurising the situation, focusing on his life in God, maybe

deliberately planning to spend time in other ways when he knows he is especially tempted. At university there is no shortage of alternatives.

3. Memorising key verses will be of help (Psa. 119:11). The beauty of becoming a Christian on campus is that he has time to get into spiritual disciplines early on. There will be days when there are no lectures until 10 am, so a leisurely breakfast followed by time reading the Bible and praying is not difficult.

4. But in all this he isn't alone. Surprise, surprise, other men have this problem and if Dave isn't in a church or group that studiously avoids any real problems, then he will find support and he may find that he is even able to support others as he is honest about his struggles.

5. At university he has a great opportunity to 'enter the drama', especially because people know his 'before and after' life. This means learning about his faith and working through books that help him get to grips with the modern challenges to Christianity. There are guys on his course and in his basketball team who are sceptical about his 'conversion' initially but who might be happy to chat.

6. He will need to integrate his faith with his course. Is it right that profit dictates business life so much? Does he really want to work for a multinational corporation that used slave labour in the two-thirds world to make its products? On the other hand, doesn't the corporate world need Christians to put forward alternative arguments?

Do you have a pattern of behaviour similar to Dave? How do you need to think and act?

Evelyn eyes models

Evelyn had a love–hate relationship with *Hello* magazine. She loved the escapism of reading about celebrities but it also reminded her of what had gone wrong in her own life. At eighteen she had the world at her feet and was often mistaken for Naomi Campbell. She had modelling offers when she finished high school and boys queuing up to ask her out. Now at thirty-two she believed the four stone she had put on meant no one would look at her and in any case she had barely any energy if anyone did! Her four children, aged four, seven, nine and twelve saw to that. She had joked that she was going to paint the words 'Taxi' on her old Peugeot 504. If she wasn't picking the children up from school she was dropping them off for evening sport, music lessons or sleepovers. She had told herself when her husband had left, that the children wouldn't suffer, but giving in to them had been very wearing, and she feared them growing up and leaving her.

Her faith helped. She prayed and enjoyed the hour on Sunday when the children were catered for at church and she could enjoy the inspirational worship at the 800-member church she attended in south London. But she thought that people didn't quite accept her. She had only been a Christian for four years, having come to faith soon after the birth of their last child. When she divorced she felt the church treated her like someone with a contagious disease. So she prayed daily and kept herself to herself and tried to get through each day. Much as she hated her extra weight, the Galaxy chocolate bars seemed to make life that much easier.

Living God's story

Evelyn is caught in a number of negative spirals. Life has been hard and so she has tried to deal with the pain. Food is a great short-term fix, which she can consume without going into debt, even with a large family. Running a family on her own is exhausting and her church is not especially supportive. To comfort herself she eats chocolate.

Chocolate is not, of course, a sin (however people want to portray it!). And being overweight is not a sin. But if it is a symptom of other problems, then it needs looking at. Her self-esteem needn't be tied to her image, but overeating and lack of exercise stem from other routes.

1. Evelyn needs to learn how to feed herself spiritually. With a young family, time alone won't be easy and there may be days when she might finish the day realising she has said little to God. But there are ways around this. There is a playgroup where she could leave the younger children one morning a week. This could become her God-time. In spite of *Hello*, she is not a keen reader so maybe she could find some way to listen to the Bible being read via an iPod, CD player or over the Internet, while doing domestic duties.

2. The spiritual food is not merely a religious exercise but her seeing herself as God sees her: as a new child in Christ, who is invited to become like Jesus. She could do all sorts of things to reduce weight but if her current image of who she is remains intact, the overeating will simply be replaced by something else! Her identity is as an apprentice of Jesus seeking to become like Jesus. He is the 'celebrity' she needs to get to know! He has the means of making radical changes to her thinking as she begins to see herself as a child of God, indwelt by the Spirit and able, through daily nurture by prayer and listening to the Bible, to see progress.

3. Her antagonism towards church needs to be overcome. Do people really have a downer on her, or is it imagined? Maybe she could join a small group within the church, which would help her get to know people properly. She might even find others who are divorced too.

4. In Evelyn's situation, life is very focused on family and problems. But as Evelyn understands that Jesus meets her in the life she is now living (not another one she might imagine) she can see her life with her children as part of her 'entering the drama'. She has opportunities to love them, care for them, nurture them, provide opportunities for them to know Jesus too, and in knowing Him, trust Him for themselves. The establishment of four lives in the

ways of God is no small ministry.

Do you have behaviour patterns that indicate something is wrong 'inside'? How can you get help?

Robert loses it

Robert was made redundant from managing a feed mill for a company that manufactured feeding stuffs for the farming industry. As foot and mouth disease decimated the beef industry and EC milk quotas changed the face of dairy farming, and the government seemed perfectly happy to see cheap imports flood the market, he had seen farming decline to the point where a feed mill the size of his became uneconomic. When head office gave him notice of closure he was not surprised. Although he had six months to close down the plant and, theoretically, find something else, he knew he would struggle. He was fifty-six, too old to retrain, too specialist in his skill-set to easily transfer to another industry. In his home in Gloucestershire, there were few alternatives and his family were settled. Having married relatively late (at forty-one) his children were still at school and he had no desire to uproot them, especially as his wife ran a thriving home design business. So they wouldn't starve, but he still had the future to face.

In truth, Robert's old story was still being lived; if he was living God's story at all he had given up at the contents page! He had been a Christian since his late teens but always kept God at arm's length. Fellow staff members knew he attended church, but were relieved that he didn't ram it down their throats, and at office parties he was known to have a few too many – he was one of the lads. He wasn't badly paid and so he and a friend invested heavily in a racehorse hoping that it might provide both enjoyment and an investment for their retirement years. But the horse fell and damaged its leg after they had owned it for a year and they had to sell it at a loss.

Robert had made some commitment to Christ but was still in first gear spiritually. He had basically carried on writing most of his own story his way and was forced to rationalise those parts of the Bible that described a style of Christianity he was not familiar with. In short, he was a dead weight in the kingdom, despite being a high-flying manager in his business. His home and marriage looked great, but inside he was full of sadness. And so he had filled life with other pleasures. Unable to drink from the fountain of pure spring water, he had gone for effluent.

Living God's story

Robert is not untypical of many who try and write the old story alongside the new. In his case the problem is poor Bible teaching that has focused on getting people 'saved' but with little or no concern to help people grow. He has concluded that Christianity is about staying out of trouble and doing your religious bit. Robert has no vision of what living in and under God's rule means, and so no vision of the Robert in Christ that God has.

This crisis moment in Robert's life can be a chance to change and progress. A number of things need to happen.

1. He needs to get a glimpse of what a life in God can be like. He may be a believer, but the Holy Spirit is banished to the 'cupboard under the stairs' within his life. Where will he get a glimpse of this? This could come from his times in church – many have been in deadish churches and have suddenly been gripped by the reality of the truth they are singing about and listening to. But the vision is more likely to come from outside: via a book; a friend who senses that all is not well and can chat with him; or a conference he attends.

2. He needs to find Christians who can model a life in God that makes sense in the twenty-first century. If you are stuck in a group of people whose mind-set is in one direction it is very hard to imagine anything different. These Christians need to be sufficiently accepting to help him grow without him feeling 'got at' for his apathy. It is hard to 'put yourself' into it (self-denial) when you fear that you will be made to feel foolish. Sane, confident, gentle Christians could help him see his potential in God and change his thinking about his role (currently non-role) in the kingdom.

3. He needs to learn to receive direction from Jesus as His child, not just in terms of 'how to find a job' but in cultivating an openness to Him in the whole of life. He needs to see that power is not about size of salary or ability to effect change in small areas, but about knowing God, being filled with Him and seeing Him effect changes in the lives of those we know.

4. His wife has a key role to play. Maybe she has a deeper faith than him and this job loss will be something God uses to bring them together. Her love, acceptance and support will be key as his self-esteem plummets during the period out of work. Often times of pain and suffering can lead us to a new seeking for God.

But people like Robert, who have been inoculated against the 'real Christianity' that Jesus offers, can be the hardest to move. There are hundreds of thousands who think they know what Jesus offers but grasp just a very small percentage. They are like plane passengers who assume they are on the plane to take a short trip around the runway. It's time for take-off.

Do you know anyone like Robert? How could you serve him/her?

Solo Rachel

Rachel was an estate agent. She loved it mostly: new people to meet and interesting homes to view. But she felt as if she lived two lives. The outgoing 'you are just going to love this place' estate agent in the day and the lonely 'I'm bored' singleton in the evenings, watching other people having fun on the TV. In fact some weeks she went the whole week without talking to anyone except her mother on the phone. Reasons for her insularity were manifold: she broke up with a guy she thought she would marry when she was twenty-one and took a year to get over it. So she became very careful how much she gave away. Her church seems so full of 'anorak types', she was never close to going out with anyone else, let alone getting close. And most of the time she was too exhausted from a day with clients to do much more than cook and slump in front of the box.

So when the alarm thrust her into the day at 7am, she filled her mind with what she had to do, knowing that the market was competitive and that if she didn't do a job for her clients someone else would. And she secretly dreaded going to homes that she would find ideal for herself, and meeting couples that were happy and in love and setting up home together. The pregnant mums were the worst, gleefully describing what they would do with each room in readiness for their growing tribe.

Church on Sunday was OK. She liked the minister who, although also single, seemed to be thoroughly OK with his situation. But this was not a church that did a great deal. About one hundred gathered each week and she was normally in the car to return home ten minutes after the end of the service. If she had spoken with two other people it would be unusual. The midweek prayer meeting was attended by the stalwarts at the church and on the few occasions she had attended she was so bored, she wondered why she bothered. But when she got down and fed up she consoled herself that she was really lucky. She was a Christian who was going to heaven and then all would be well. But was that really living her part in God's story? Clearly not.

Living God's story
Women outnumber men in the Western Church so there are likely to be many women who won't find a Christian partner and many, like Rachel, whose faith is tested by this. But although she may think her singleness is top of the agenda, the truth is that her faith – and consequently her lifestyle – is.

She doesn't see her work as part of her life in Christ. It is an inconvenience – good sometimes, bad sometimes – and has little or no connection with her Christian life, apart from allowing her to give money to the church. The problem is not that Rachel doesn't 'take God to work' but that her relationship with God is such that she doesn't give Him a thought at work. If life in Christ is learning to live her life as Jesus would, she needs to make changes.

1. There is nothing in her life that gives God a look in outside of a Sunday service. She needs to set the alarm earlier so that she has time to pray through the day before it starts. Or if that seems too

burdensome, schedule a time with God after she has eaten in the evening. Only when her thinking about God and herself changes will she be able to change. She mustn't see this as a 'religious exercise' and certainly not a means of bargaining with God to give her a man. This is as key as breakfast, a chance to remind herself that she is a follower of Jesus, who will lead her into each day and enable her to thrive even when life has not been kind.

2. Her jealousy of pregnant women and happy couples won't disappear overnight, but she needs to recognise that it must go eventually. She might feel justified in these emotions, but it is hard to be jealous and want the good of another (the Bible's definition of love). What about asking God to change her attitude towards pregnant women and happy couples?

3. If church isn't too hot socially maybe she can offer to set something up herself? Maybe others feel like she does. And she certainly has the personality to welcome new people. There again, if the church is doing little to help her develop her understanding of her faith, and she talks to almost no one, maybe it is time to move churches? In short, if there isn't a bit more action in her life, she will be prey to spending more years just going through the motions when she has gifts and talents that God is keen to use, if only she will find the right environment and make the decision to do so. God will not do it for her. She's a big girl and He's looking for her to seek Him, knowing that if she does He has loads to show her and excite her.

4. Instead of fearing meeting pregnant couples, she would be better praying for every client, that they may be blessed by God.

5. Praying for a life partner is important but needs to be supplemented with a decision not to dwell on it. Wanting to be married is a legitimate desire, but a person who makes being married their prime concern is tempted to put their life on hold until the desire is fulfilled. Rachel needs to release the thinking

and accept that if she is to be single for the rest of her life, that is fine, even if it wouldn't be her choice or desire. God would enable her to fill her life appropriately, she doesn't need to accept the norms of the world (and sometimes the Church) that single = sad. Jesus and Paul – to name but two – would say otherwise.

Who do you know who is single? How can you support them better?

Four people, each of whom are discovering their part in God's story, all with struggles and challenges – none of them beyond God's help if they are prepared to get intentional about following Jesus daily and learning from Him. As you read through their situations, you may have, at times, felt connected to them. Are you facing similar challenges? Are you doing any better? It is often said that 'life is not a dress rehearsal'! There is some truth in that, although those who say it often presume that you get nothing more than the years you are given on earth. As you learn from Jesus, He will give you perspectives and outlooks that will change you and make you desperate to see your life and the lives of others turned right around. It's time to make sure that the old story script you have in your head really is replaced by God's.

Summary

1. We need to imagine what life in the kingdom might look like.
2. We face various challenges in life, but putting our confidence in Jesus will enable us to transform them. In the case of each of these examples, it is possible to imagine 'living God's story', but action based on a true assessment of life is necessary. God will do it, but He won't do it without you.
3. You have the opportunity to enjoy God's story, now. What's stopping you?

Action

1. Read back over the characters' situations. Where are the similarities with you? Are there things you need to do?
2. As you have almost finished the book, list five things you are going to do as a result of what you have read.
3. Is there anything you can tell a friend from what you have read?

Consider

1. Who do you know who really lives their part in God's story? Can you ask them to share their secrets?
2. What is your best guess at what God wants you to do with your life as result of what you have been reading?

FINALE

When I was sharing a house in Reading in 1989, my housemate arrived home excited one evening.

'I have just watched a film that understands me,' he announced.

Guessing that he didn't quite mean exactly what he had just said, I asked him, 'How come?'

He tried to explain how absolutely brilliant the film was – but as they say, 'you had to be there'.

It wasn't until I actually saw *Dead Poets Society* that I understood. The film is set in an American all-boys baording school and focuses on the counter-cultural way one of the English tutors, Professor Keating, played by Robin Williams, encourages his class to value each and every day, inspired by poets like Walt Whitman who encouraged a bold approach to life. His favourite phrase was *'carpe diem'* – Latin for 'seize the day', which encouraged the pupils to go against the status quo. It was my housemate's philosophy – make the very most of every day, fit in all you can. If you visit a town and can drop in on a friend, do so; if you can use a business trip to also visit the theatre do so. Maximise every day as much as you can. It was at times exhausting to live with but, having seen the film, I understood why he felt the film resonated so strongly.

The 'seize the day' philosophy actually comes from humanist roots. You have to seize the day because you only have 'this life'. It is the 'eat, drink and be merry for tomorrow we die' mentality. But you can also adopt the 'seize the day' philosophy the way my friend did, realising that each day is a precious gift from God. Spend it carefully.

The end of any book provides opportunities to 'seize the day'. If the time spent reading is not to be wasted, it is worth spending some time now – or very soon – reflecting on what difference the information is going to make to you. Perhaps there were some 'aha' moments, or 'must investigate that' times?

There are some simple ways in which you can maximise your reading:

1. Go back over the summary points of each chapter and highlight any parts you want to re-read. This may take less than twenty minutes.

2. You might want to look at any sections requiring action, or answers, and determine to work them through.

3. If there are actions, then writing them down helps you towards completing them. Giving yourself a deadline and telling someone you have done so will ensure that you do what you intend.

It may just be one thing that will make a big difference.

Remember, God is good, He is kind, He is generous and He has lots for you to know and experience.

He graciously waits for your responses to His truth. He likes nothing better than to draw near to those who call on Him. And He longs that you may know the riches of His grace in this life until the day when faith gives way to sight and you see and know Him in all His beauty and glory.

He is very gracious and gentle and will not intrude if He is not wanted.

Jesus is looking to lead you in your life – in a life to die for. Nothing phases Him. You can start now, right where you are. You have a part to play in God's story – what exactly is it that is more important?

Remember, God's story does not have a happy ending. That's because it doesn't end! For at the end of every chapter appear the words: To Be Continued …

Continue well.

If you have any comments or queries you can contact me at andynicpeck@bigfoot.com

APPENDIX

The specifics of God's story

A story which includes 783,000 words is daunting.

The following diagrams will help you grasp the major elements, with just a few numbers to learn.

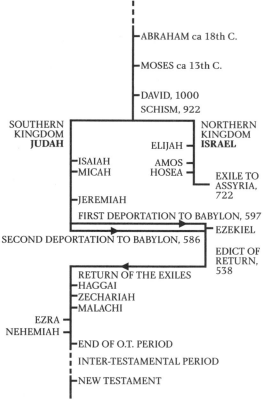

Outline of Old Testament History (Not to scale)

Adapted from: G. Goldsworthy, *Gospel and Kingdom* (Paternoster, 1981), p.33.
Used by permission.

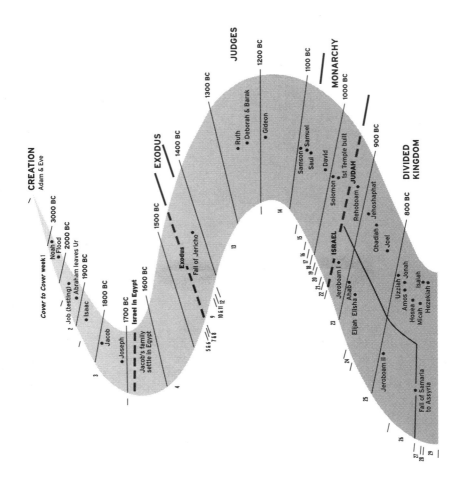

Taken from Selwyn Hughes and Trevor Partridge, *Cover to Cover Complete* (CWR, 2007) pp.10–11. This time chart is based on *The Reese Chronological Bible* edited by Edward Reese.

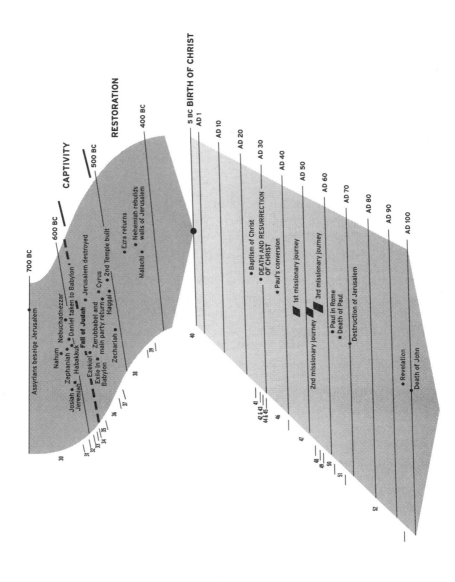

CAPTIVITY

RESTORATION

700 BC

600 BC

500 BC

400 BC

Assyrians besiege Jerusalem

Nahum   Nebuchadnezzar

Josiah •   Zephaniah •   • Daniel taken to Babylon   • Jerusalem destroyed
Jeremiah •   Habakkuk •   Fall of Judah

Ezekiel •   Zerubbabel and   • Cyrus
Exile in   main party return •   Haggai •   • 2nd Temple built
Babylon
                    Zechariah •

• Ezra returns

Malachi •   • Nehemiah rebuilds
            walls of Jerusalem

30   31   32   33   34   35   36   37   38   39

5 BC BIRTH OF CHRIST
AD 1

AD 10

AD 20

AD 30

AD 40

AD 50

AD 60

AD 70

AD 80

AD 90

AD 100

• Baptism of Christ

DEATH AND RESURRECTION
OF CHRIST

• Paul's conversion

1st missionary journey

2nd missionary journey
3rd missionary journey

• Paul in Rome
• Death of Paul

Destruction of Jerusalem

• Revelation

• Death of John

40   41   42 & 43   44 & 45   46   47   48   49   50   51   52

NATIONAL DISTRIBUTORS

UK: (and countries not listed below)
CWR, Waverley Abbey House, Waverley Lane, Farnham, Surrey GU9 8EP.
Tel: (01252) 784700 Outside UK (44) 1252 784700

AUSTRALIA: CMC Australasia, PO Box 519, Belmont, Victoria 3216.
Tel: (03) 5241 3288 Fax: (03) 5241 3290

CANADA: Cook Communications Ministries, PO Box 98, 55 Woodslee Avenue,
Paris, Ontario N3L 3E5. Tel: 1800 263 2664

GHANA: Challenge Enterprises of Ghana, PO Box 5723, Accra.
Tel: (021) 222437/223249 Fax: (021) 226227

HONG KONG: Cross Communications Ltd, 1/F, 562A Nathan Road, Kowloon.
Tel: 2780 1188 Fax: 2770 6229

INDIA: Crystal Communications, 10-3-18/4/1, East Marredpalli, Secunderabad
– 500026, Andhra Pradesh. Tel/Fax: (040) 27737145

KENYA: Keswick Books and Gifts Ltd, PO Box 10242, Nairobi.
Tel: (02) 331692/226047 Fax: (02) 728557

MALAYSIA: Salvation Book Centre (M) Sdn Bhd, 23 Jalan SS 2/64,
47300 Petaling Jaya, Selangor.
Tel: (03) 78766411/78766797 Fax: (03) 78757066/78756360

NEW ZEALAND: CMC Australasia, PO Box 303298, North Harbour,
Auckland 0751. Tel: 0800 449 408 Fax: 0800 449 049

NIGERIA: FBFM, Helen Baugh House, 96 St Finbarr's College Road,
Akoka, Lagos. Tel: (01) 7747429/4700218/825775/827264

PHILIPPINES: OMF Literature Inc, 776 Boni Avenue, Mandaluyong City.
Tel: (02) 531 2183 Fax: (02) 531 1960

SINGAPORE: Alby Commercial Enterprises Pte Ltd, 95 Kallang Avenue #04-
00, AIS Industrial Building, 339420. Tel: (65) 629 27238 Fax: (65) 629 27235

SOUTH AFRICA: Struik Christian Books, 80 MacKenzie Street, PO Box 1144,
Cape Town 8000. Tel: (021) 462 4360 Fax: (021) 461 3612

SRI LANKA: Christombu Publications (Pvt) Ltd, Bartleet House, 65 Braybrooke
Place, Colombo 2. Tel: (9411) 2421073/2447665

TANZANIA: CLC Christian Book Centre, PO Box 1384, Mkwepu Street,
Dar es Salaam. Tel/Fax: (022) 2119439

USA: Cook Communications Ministries, PO Box 98, 55 Woodslee Avenue, Paris,
Ontario N3L 3E5, Canada. Tel: 1800 263 2664

ZIMBABWE: Word of Life Books (Pvt) Ltd, Christian Media Centre, 8 Aberdeen
Road, Avondale, PO Box A480 Avondale, Harare.
Tel: (04) 333355 or 091301188

For email addresses, visit the CWR website: www.cwr.org.uk
CWR is a Registered Charity – Number 294387
CWR is a Limited Company registered in England – Registration Number
1990308

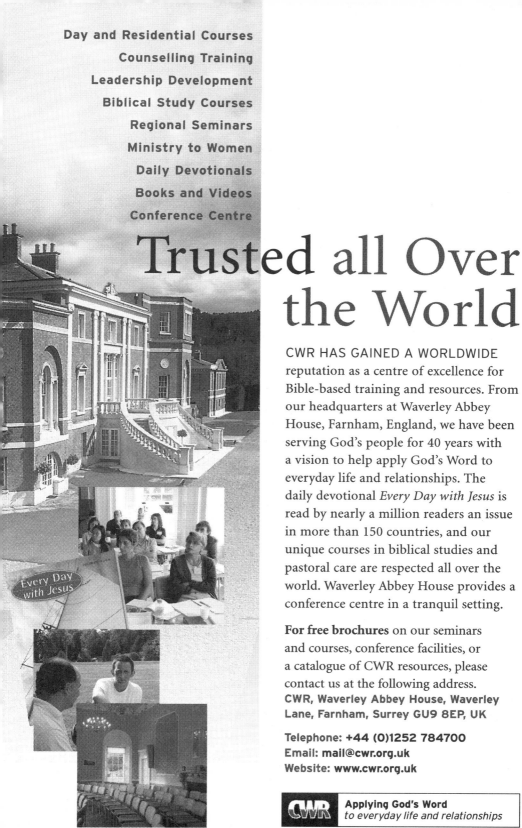

Day and Residential Courses
Counselling Training
Leadership Development
Biblical Study Courses
Regional Seminars
Ministry to Women
Daily Devotionals
Books and Videos
Conference Centre

Trusted all Over the World

CWR HAS GAINED A WORLDWIDE reputation as a centre of excellence for Bible-based training and resources. From our headquarters at Waverley Abbey House, Farnham, England, we have been serving God's people for 40 years with a vision to help apply God's Word to everyday life and relationships. The daily devotional *Every Day with Jesus* is read by nearly a million readers an issue in more than 150 countries, and our unique courses in biblical studies and pastoral care are respected all over the world. Waverley Abbey House provides a conference centre in a tranquil setting.

For free brochures on our seminars and courses, conference facilities, or a catalogue of CWR resources, please contact us at the following address.
CWR, Waverley Abbey House, Waverley Lane, Farnham, Surrey GU9 8EP, UK

Telephone: **+44 (0)1252 784700**
Email: **mail@cwr.org.uk**
Website: **www.cwr.org.uk**

 Applying God's Word
to everyday life and relationships

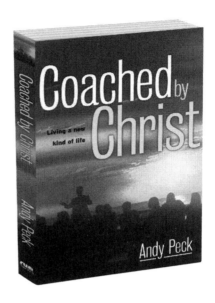

COACHED BY CHRIST

This book shows us how we can put ourselves in the hands of the greatest coach in the universe – Christ Himself. If we can learn from His way, He will work with us and is the model for what the author has called the 'new kind of life'.

£7.99 (plus p&p)
ISBN: 978-1-85345-348-9
Price correct at time of printing.

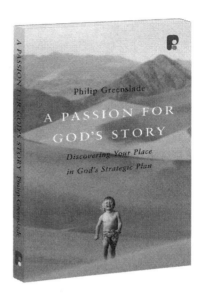

A PASSION FOR GOD'S STORY

Discover your place in God's strategic plan! This book is nothing less than the Big Story of 'what on earth God is doing'. It shows how the Bible tells of God's covenants with mankind as part of His redemptive plan, the ultimate goal of which is the new creation.

£9.99 (plus p&p)
ISBN: 978-1-84227-094-3
Price correct at time of printing.

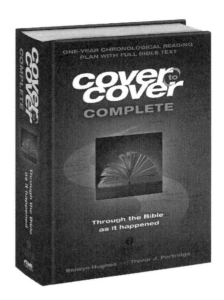

COVER TO COVER COMPLETE

Packed into this single volume is everything you need for a thrilling chronological voyage of discovery through the whole Bible as it happened. Based on the original acclaimed reading plan, *Cover to Cover*, this complete volume includes:

• charts, maps, illustrations and diagrams
• a timeline on every page
• devotional thoughts for contemplation each day
• and – for the first time – the complete Bible text.

There is also a related website featuring character studies, readers' testimonies, helpful hints and much more.

£19.99 (plus p&p)
Special introductory offer: £17.99 (until 31 December 2007)
ISBN: 978-1-85345-433-2
Price correct at time of printing.